TRUTHBOMBS:

BRIEF THOUGHTS ON BIG ISSUES

BRAXTON HUNTER

Trinity Academic Press

Evansville, Indiana

i

Trinity Academic Press
World Wide Web: Trinitysem.edu
Email:Contact@trinitysem.edu

ISBN-13: 978-0692376201 (Custom)
ISBN-10: 0692376208

Printed in the United States of America

For Harold F. Hunter
Dropping Truthbombs on my life
since 1980

CONTENTS

INTRODUCTION   vii

CHRISTIAN LIVING

WE DIDN'T LIKE CHURCH SO WE WENT TO WALMART   2

3 PRINCIPLES FOR BECOMING A MORE PRODUCTIVE
MINISTRY LEADER   9

THE EARLY CHURCH AND APPLE COMPUTERS   18

IS HAPPINESS THE TRUTH: VICTORIA OSTEEN,
PHARRELL WILLIAMS AND FREAKONOMICS   24

MY THOUGHTS ON HAVING ANOTHER GIRL   30

AMBER-ALERT AT THE LOCAL STARBUCKS   35

5 PRACTICAL WAYS TO GROW IN KNOWLEDGE FAST   40

DISTORTING DEFOE: HOW HOLLYWOOD SHIPWRECKED
CRUSOE'S ONLY HOPE   45

F18S, PREACHING AND THE DEFENSE OF THE FAITH   48

3 THINGS YOU HAVE TO REALIZE RIGHT NOW   54

APOLOGETICS

MOPEDS AND MORALITY: A REALLY SHORT STORY   60

THE MEANING OF LIFE   66

WASN'T THE NEW TESTAMENT JUST WRITTEN BY
BIASED CHRISTIANS?   72

TWO THINGS PRO-CHOICE ADVOCATES NEED TO HEAR   75

WHO MADE GOD?   85

GEEK GOD DENIES GOD: SCI-FI HERO STEPHEN
HAWKING TRIES TO MAKE GOD "REDUNDANT"   88

WHEN ORGANIZED RELIGION IS A PROBLEM: MUSLIMS
AND METHODISTS IN BIBLE/KORAN COLLEGE TOGETHER 96

4 REASONS SCIENCE IS NOT AT ODDS WITH RELIGION 102

5 REASONS THINKING CHRISTIANS DON'T AFFIRM
OPPOSING WORLD VIEWS   109

HOW MANY ATHEISTS DOES IT TAKE TO PUT UP A
BILLBOARD   116

THEOLOGY

3 VIEWS ON HELL   122

MIRACLES   128

WHAT'S UP WITH OLD TESTAMENT SACRIFICES?   132

HOW DOES THE TRINITY WORK?   136

ANGELS AND DEMONS   139

HOW NOT TO TREAT THE BIBLE   143

TALKING PAST EACH OTHER: ONE ISSUE ABOUT THE
CALVINISM DEBATE THAT CHRISTIANS MISUNDERSTAND 151

BLACK MAGIC: A MINOR APOLOGETIC ANNOYANCE
ABOUT THE SOTERIOLOGY DEBATE   157

TALKING PAST EACH OTHER PART 2 (LOVE)   161

SANTA TEACHES THEOLOGY   169

EVANGELISM

SHOULD MINISTERS STILL EXTEND "DECISIONAL
INVITATIONS?"   174

DO ATHEISTS EXIST: EVANGELISM ON FOX'S NEW
SHOW UTOPIA   183

3 WAYS THE CHURCH SHOULD VIEW ISIS   188

3 THINGS YOUR CHRISTIAN BELIEFS SHOULD CHANGE 194

WHAT WOULD THE MARTYRS SAY: MY BELATED FOLLOW-
UP TO THE WWJD CRAZE   198

INTRODUCTION

Truth according to Merriam-Webster is defined as, "The real facts about something." The definition of "bomb" is, "An explosive device fused to detonate under specific conditions." Thus, we might define a truth-bomb as, "An explosive fused to detonate the real facts about things under certain conditions." Wiring truthbombs has been my desire and goal for several years now. There is so much falsehood and confusion in the 21st century that Christians need to have these explosive devices in their arsenals for when the enemy attacks. This book represents what we might think of as a cache of such devices to pick up, and run with, in the midst of spiritual warfare.

What you will find here is not comprehensive. My other books were written in a cohesive manner to address specific issues that arise for Christians. *Truthbombs* is an eclectic collection of blog articles and leftovers from previous projects. It is not necessarily intended to be read straight through, although it wouldn't take long. Instead, I recognize that we live in a fast-paced world and not everyone has the time or attention span to read a long apologetics book (let's be honest with ourselves). Some people have a hard time getting through a single ten-page chapter (you know who you are). If this hits home, I put this together for you. Merry Christmas. There are even a couple of chapters on Christmas, come to think of it. Likewise, you'll find chapters on theology, church, atheism, Islam, Christian living, celebrities, leadership, bible study, music, miracles and a lot of other stuff.

By the way, expect some dated material. As some of this was originally written in 2009 there are references to people who are actually already dead. Cultural issues are discussed that have already faded in your memory. Whoops. You might ask, "Why didn't you just cut those things out?" This is a reasonable question, but I think the issues expressed even in those chapters are still relevant. Besides, this is a raw and uncut collection of articles that would have otherwise ended up on the cutting room floor. Think of them as B-sides (a dated term, I know) or deleted scenes. And I know what you're thinking. Just like a musician putting out a record of rare and unreleased tracks, isn't this self-indulgent? I don't think so.

I'm no great writer. For that matter, I'm not the greatest living evangelist, or Christian apologist. Yet, these are writings that others have found helpful. I'm always humbled and surprised to hear this, but it is true. If God has given me anything worth saying, I'm going to say it.

My motto is, "Get up and do something!" A few years ago I got a membership to a local gym. The men's locker room also had a steam room. Relaxing after a hard workout in the steam room was my daily reward for powering through my regiment. With dread, though, I remember the day that I glanced at the door to the inviting sweat tank and saw the clouds of moisture billowing out in an inviting way. I thought, "Maybe just today, I won't work out. Maybe just today, I'll just go into the steam room." Big mistake! The steam room was populated by out of shape men. They were extremely knowledgeable out of shape men. The steam room fellas could tell you everything you needed to know about effective fitness strategies. All the terminology was there. No one could argue with their advice. To say they knew what they were talking about would be an understatement. In fact, I discovered another benefit to joining the steam room club. After you leave the steam room you look as though you really went to the gym and, "killed it!" Sweat continued to flow readily for a good thirty minutes after I would leave and my skin retained a pinkish hue as if I had worked out . . . hard. Simply put, I had the look of a man who was doing something, I had the know-how and I received all the acclaim from friends and family for a hard work out. The problem, as I realized, was that nothing changed. We had talked quite a bit, but we hadn't done anything.

Often Christians have all the knowledge and the look of someone who is really "killing it," so to speak. The problem is that they aren't doing anything. I want to get up and do something for God. I don't want to let a single helpful thought or opportunity go unnoticed. Not only do I want to do something that matters for the Lord, I want you to do something. Take these simple articles for what they are and use them where you can. If you have something to say, let this inspire you to start your own blog, or write your own book. Christianity today is in need of talented authors, thinkers and evangelists. Maybe in the midst of reading this material you will begin to wire your own truthbombs!

CHRISTIAN LIVING

THE MATERIAL IN THIS SECTION IS
INTENDED TO ASSIST BELIEVERS IN
LIVING OUT THE CHRISTIAN LIFE IN A
VICTORIOUS WAY. IT IS MY HOPE THAT
YOU WILL BENEFIT GREATLY FROM MOVING
THROUGH THESE CHAPTERS. FEEL FREE TO
SKIP AROUND. EACH ARTICLE IS ITS OWN
THING. THEY DO NOT BUILD ON EACH
OTHER. USE THEM AS DEVOTIONAL
MATERIAL OR JUST TO PASS THE TIME.
MANY OF THEM ARE STILL POSTED ON MY
MINISTRY WEBSITE. I WOULD LOVE TO
INTERACT WITH YOU ABOUT THEM THERE
IF YOU WANT TO SHARE YOUR THOUGHTS.
MINISTRY LEADERS AND ACADEMICS OFTEN
OVERLOOK WHAT WE CALL CHRISTIAN
LIVING MATERIAL. NEVERTHELESS, OUR
GROWTH IN THIS AREA IS AS IMPORTANT
AS ANY OTHER. I ENCOURAGE BELIEVERS
OF EVERY KIND TO LET THESE
TRUTHBOMBS IMAPACT THEIR LIVES TOO.

WE DIDN'T LIKE CHURCH SO WE WENT TO WALMART

DISCLAIMER: *A number of people don't like, or go to, Walmart for a number of political and ethical reasons. If that is the case, then just insert Target, Ikea, gas stations or most any discount store in place of Walmart. If you think I'm making fun of, or criticizing, Walmart you should know I shop there regularly.*

As I consider the reasons I most often hear for why "Jane Christian" doesn't go to church, I have noticed that on those same premises "Jane Christian" should also never go to *Walmart* (or almost anywhere). The *North American Mission Board* of the *Southern Baptist Convention* met this week, in Atlanta, for their *Summer State Leadership Meeting.* As the new president of the *Conference of Southern Baptist Evangelists* (COSBE), I was in attendance. As I heard one report after another I was reminded of the fact that "Jane" (not a specific person, but a name I am using to indicate former churchgoers) is not coming to church and is prepared to tell you why. As we consider some of her reasons, I am asking you to notice how they would, were Jane consistent, lead her away from a number of other institutions (namely, *Walmart*). In fact, I almost titled this article, *If you left church because of the hypocrites, then you're a hypocrite to go to Walmart.*"

Church is full of hypocrites

Last week as I was preaching in Evansville, In, A woman made a prayer request which involved her son, who doesn't go to church because he alleges that it contains a number of hypocrites. Since this is one of the most popular claims "Jane Christian" makes lets take a look at it. If you put the argument formally it would look like this:

1) If hypocrites are at church, I shouldn't go to church,

2) Hypocrites are at church, thus

3) I shouldn't go to church.

Indeed we can all agree with Jane that it is the case that there are hypocrites at church. There is no getting around it. I know some of them. I'll go a step further. At some point I have probably been the church hypocrite. What is problematic is that one could make the same claim about people who shop at *Walmart*. Then Jane's argument would just look like this:

1) If hypocrites are at *Walmart*, I shouldn't go to *Walmart*,

2) Hypocrites are at *Walmart*, thus

3) I shouldn't go to *Walmart*.

So if Jane won't go to church, and she is going to be consistent (not a hypocrite herself), Jane can't go to *Walmart*. The only way to refute this is to show that there are not hypocrites at *Walmart*, or that there is something more valuable at *Walmart* that demands that Jane puts up with hypocrites in order to get it.

Well, unless plastic swimming-pools, pizza-rolls, *Twilight* posters, toilet-paper or fish-tanks are more important than the creator of the universe and his community of believers, then there is nothing better at *Walmart* that would demand Jane's putting up with hypocrisy there if she doesn't at church. It would also be silly to argue that there are no hypocrites at *Walmart*. After all, most of the hypocrites at church are also at *Walmart*. Furthermore, any place where you are likely to find a full-blown *McDonald's* a stone's throw from diet pills and workout equipment is bound to be a haven for hypocrites. So unless Jane wants to be a hypocrite herself then she must give up on the idea that she is justified in not going to church because of the presence of hypocrites. Yet, Jane has more to say.

I don't fit in

She might claim that people at church are not enough like herself. That claim would look like this:

1) I don't go where people are not like me.

2) People at church are not like me, thus

3) I don't go to church.

Naturally, premise two is correct. There are undoubtedly a number of people at church not like Jane. This is true no matter who Jane is. Why? There are all kinds of people at church. Here's the problem. Just as before, the same argument Jane used above could be ascribed to *Walmart*. So in order for Jane's reasoning to stand, she must show that everyone at *Walmart* is like her (or at least enough like her that she is comfortable). However, this is absurd since the very people she is not enough like at church probably shop at *Walmart*. Since Jane will likely be unable to demonstrate that she is more like these people than those in her church, she cannot use this argument without rendering herself a hypocrite. Ever relentless, Jane has more to say.

Untrustworthy ministers

She could argue that ministers cannot be trusted because of moral failings. That argument would go like this:

1) If ministers are untrustworthy I shouldn't go to church,

2) Some ministers are untrustworthy, thus

3) I shouldn't go to church.

This argument has been all the rage for the past 25 or 30 years. And Jane is right that there are untrustworthy ministers in the world. Yet, if she makes this claim she cannot go to *Walmart* without being a hypocrite. First, she is much more likely to encounter an untrustworthy minister at *Walmart* than at her church. Why? Jane's local church, depending on size, will likely have less than a handful of ordained ministers. If they are trustworthy then

Jane can feel comfortable. On the other hand, every minister in the community, as well as ministers passing through the community, visits *Walmart*. This means that, probabilistically, there is a greater chance Jane will encounter an untrustworthy minister at *Walmart* than at her local church. So on the argument above, Jane should never go to *Walmart*.

A word should be said about the trustworthiness of ministers. I have now been in full-time evangelism for 4 and one half years.[1] During that time I have only met one individual minister who was in any way untrustworthy. Even in his case, he has repented. The modern caricature of ministers as being money-hungry pedophiles will not stick. Don't play into that lie. Are there individuals who fit the bill? Absolutely. And when they are found out, the church shouts the loudest.

In conclusion

It is true of a lot of believers that they will not go to church, but they regularly go to *Walmart*, *Target*, *Kmart*, malls, gas stations,

---

[1] At the time of the publishing of this book, I have been in evangelism for 9 years and what I say here is still true.

Ikeas and a number of other places whose names could have been inserted in place of *Walmart's*. Ultimately, since we have seen that Jane's arguments will not work, there must be some other reason she resists the sacred practice of fellowship and community in local church bodies. Perhaps it is because someone hurt her feelings. Indeed my feelings have been hurt at *Walmart* when I couldn't fit into size 32″ jeans. Maybe, she simply doesn't want to spend the time, or doesn't see the point. Nevertheless, I urge believers to share these thoughts with Christians who have drifted away and urge them with love. Making a clever point about how they are inconsistent will be meaningless if we do not also show them that we care at least as much as do the *Walmart* employees. The truth is that what God offers the world through the body of Christ is more valuable than anything at *Walmart*. It didn't come at "everyday low prices" but Christ died to purchase it for Jane.

3 PRINCIPLES FOR BECOMING A MORE PRODUCTIVE MINISTRY LEADER

Utter apathy! That was my feeling as I sat there running my index finger around the circumference of my plastic water bottle. To my right was Roy Fish, Professor of Evangelism at *Southwestern Baptist Theological Seminary*. To my left was a seasoned veteran of evangelism. Both of these well-dressed men seemed enthusiastic about the event. Both of them had previously been asked to serve in this same capacity many times. I had not. Why was I so disinterested? After all, this would be good for my career. It would look good on a resume. My own organization would get better exposure. Yet, in the midst of all of the fanfare, I was painfully bored. It was 2010 and the Conference of Southern Baptist Evangelists (COSBE) was on the verge of electing a new president. At twenty-nine I was the second youngest member of the Southern Baptist Convention's outreach arm of itinerant speakers. I should have been thrilled to be asked to speak. I wasn't. Then it happened.

The next day it came to my attention that a campaign had already been underway behind the scenes to present me as a candidate for the presidential office. Some of those who were pressing the issue were complete strangers. By one vote, I was installed as president and a spark became a flame as my apathy dissolved. The same day I was ushered into a private banquet hall filled with the most influential leaders of America's largest evangelical denomination. Promoters paraded me around the convention and news outlets contacted me for interviews.

Once the noise faded and I was back in my hotel room I noticed an internal change. I had, within the span of twenty-four hours, become a different person. I noticed myself downloading apps designed to keep me efficient. Emails were sent out to powerbrokers I had met that day to thank them for their time. Former COSBE presidents and interested businessmen were contacted for advisory meetings. I even hit the gym. In short, I became ridiculously productive. I was a checklist-dominating master. More was accomplished during my time serving in that position than I had done in the previous five years. The question that often occurred to me was, "What on earth happened to transform my thinking from apathy to passion in less than a day?" I have determined that there were three simple principles. For these principles to exist, it may seem like the stars need to align, but once they are in place no one needs to motivate you. You will also become a checklist-dominating master of productivity. They are, POSITION, POWER and POSSIBILITY.

Position

If you aren't in the right position to do anything, then nothing is going to happen. If your in the right position, but aren't taking advantage of it, then nothing will change either. Getting into the right position, or becoming a leader is hard enough. However, there are far too many leaders that have the right position but still sit there bored, running their index fingers around the circumferences of plastic water bottles while waiting for the world to end. They aren't taking advantage of the position.

About the same time I landed the position of president at

COSBE, I also got a membership at the YMCA. The men's locker room had a steam room. Relaxing after a hard workout in the steam room was my daily reward for powering through my regiment. With dread, though, I remember the day that I glanced at the door to the inviting sweat tank and saw the clouds of moisture billowing out in an inviting way. I thought, "Maybe just today, I won't work out. Maybe just today, I'll just go into the steam room." Big mistake!

The steam room was populated by out of shape men. They were extremely knowledgeable out of shape men. The steam room fellas could tell you everything you needed to know about effective fitness strategies. All the terminology was there. No one could argue with their advice. To say they knew what they were talking about would be an understatement. In fact, I discovered another benefit to joining the steam room club. After you leave the steam room you look as though you really went to the gym and, "killed it!" Sweat continued to flow readily for a good thirty minutes after I would leave and my skin retained a pinkish hue as if I had worked out . . . hard. Simply put, I had the look of a man who was doing something, I had the know-how and I received all the acclaim from friends and family for a hard work out. The problem, as I realized, was that nothing changed. We had talked quite a bit, but we hadn't done anything.

In the same way, many leaders have the position, the look and the textbook answers to the problems they are facing. Unfortunately, like the steam room fellas, they aren't taking advantage of their positions. After a day at the office, their families and friends think they really, "killed it." Yet, what the leader may not even admit to himself, is that he has been sitting in the steam room . . . all . . . day . . . long.

Power

What if you have the position and you're willing to step out of the steam room, but you still aren't accomplishing the necessary goals? What if you still find yourself ambivalent or bored? If the willingness is really there, it may be that a given leader has not recognized or utilized the power that he has been given. As a man who has often found confrontation or boat-rocking extremely uncomfortable, I have had this problem repeatedly.

When I was pastoring my second church at the age of twenty-three, I recognized what a benefit a projection screen would be for our church sanctuary. This may seem like a small issue, but at my young age, and having heard horror stories about angry deacons who look for chances to lambast young ministers, I was nervous. I knew that I had the authority (or power) to make the decision unilaterally since my personal budget was above the cost, but I still found myself reluctant to pull the trigger. For months I hemmed and hawed at the decision. Finally, one Saturday night, under the cover of darkness, the youth minister and I made the purchase and the installation. The next morning I was an uneasy cocktail of excited and scared-silly. Deacon Dread, as I shall call him, approached the doors of the church and I stopped him with a sheepish grin. "Deacon Dread," I uttered, "I just want you to know, before you set foot in the building, that last night we installed a projector." Dread looked at the air with squinted eyes as though the word "projector" was hanging there for him to examine. Finally he looked at me and in a sturdy tone bluntly said, "Good. We voted to do that before you ever came and nobody ever followed through. Besides, you're the pastor. If you want to put up a projector . . . why . . . go for it." Success! The relief that rolled over me was liberating. Deacon Dread wasn't dreadful at all. In fact, he was deacon-down-right-agreeable. From that day I not only remained aware of, but willing to exercise, my position of power.

In a leadership position one must recognize and be willing to exercise his power. We wouldn't be given power if we were not expected to make decisions and act as an authority in one respect or other. If this is not the expectation of those who interviewed you then some serious conversations need to be had. If you've got the position, and the power, then you are two thirds of the way down the road to becoming an empowered and productive leader who is able to accomplish his goals.

Possibility

Let's return to my situation as a newly elected denominational leader. My renewed enthusiasm was not just the result of my new position and power. These two elements would have been pointless had I not also seen great potential in the organization. That potential led me to believe that there was a great possibility for success in the future. If there is no possibility for success, and let's not kid ourselves sometimes there isn't, then our leadership may inspire some onlookers, but it won't even genuinely motivate us. Some projects need to be abandoned. Some programs need to be ditched in favor of new ones. Faith in and of itself is not a good thing. Faith in a bad program is always a bad move. However, just because everyone else on your team thinks a particular project is a bad one doesn't mean that you should give up. Moreover, your early commitment to accomplish a task may lead you to innovate. You're the leader precisely because you were trusted with the power to make that call. This is why it is vitally important that you are able to be honest with yourself. Nevertheless, if the position, power and possibility is present, there is no end to what can be accomplished.

Prayer

Yes, I know. The title is "THREE Principles for Becoming a More Productive Ministry Leader." That's because I assumed that a ministry leader should already recognize the need to bathe every decision in prayer. Yet, I can not deny the tendencies of the loud-mouthed, leather-lunged, red-faced southern preacher that I am. God is the one who undergirds our ministry POSITIONS. Our POWER has the Holy Spirit for its source and in Jesus' name our impossibilities become POSSIBILITIES. Amen and amen!

THE EARLY CHURCH AND APPLE COMPUTERS

In 2005 my wife, Sarah, needed a new computer. Sitting here in 2010 I cannot remember what it was that influenced our decision to allow a paradigm shift to take place in our lives wherein she set sail from our happy home in the world of PC and embarked on the *Mac* Journey. Still a *PC* user, I could liken this to the story of what happened to Eve and her "apple" (I know, I know, - scripture doesn't specify), but the difference is that this Adam (me) doesn't eat forbidden fruit (at least not when it comes to computers). What happened in her life was indeed something like a microcosm of a conversion experience. Suddenly, we both had *iPods* instead of traditional mp3 players (okay, so I nibbled). She also started buying software for her *Apple* that wouldn't work on my *PC*. It changed the way she worked, shopped, communicated and browsed online. Even though I had been raised in the faith (from 6th through 12th grade my school used *Apple*) the new addition to her life seemed strange to me. The cursor didn't even look the same. It's amazing how changing a computer is so similar to changing a worldview. Nevertheless, as the years went on she began to slip further into the cult of *Apple* (relax. I'm just making a point). She began to make fun of my computer. She started wanting to go to church . . . I mean the *Apple* Store, and every time I had a computer problem she would say, "If you only had a *Mac*." Honestly, the same computer she got in 2005 is amazingly still running fine. It has never had a virus or major technical problem despite having been repeatedly dropped, stepped on and drenched in water.[2] What's the point?

In thirty years' time (it was started in 1976), the congregation of *Apple* disciples has grown from 0 to millions, causing them to be despised by many outside of their ranks. Surely, there are many who would love to see great harm come to the company itself. Similarly, from the time of the events surrounding Jesus' crucifixion, the church had grown to the point that the Roman tyrant, Nero, felt the

---

[2] It is now 2015 and the thing is still working.

need to persecute them. In 64 A.D. a massive fire destroyed much of Rome. Most historians feel that Nero himself caused the fire and blamed it on the Christians. From this, persecutions began, involving the violent and bloody deaths of many believers. Paul was likely one of the martyrs. The rapid growth of the church, which prompted unease on the part of Nero, took place in no more than 30-35 years. Why am I drawing this parallel?

It is partly to give you a living, modern example of what it would have been like in the first century to see a group rising to dominance quite swiftly because of something that they collectively believed in with great passion. Obviously, *Apple Computers* is no actual parallel to the glory of God and the eternal value of the body of Christ. Steve Jobs[3] cannot offer you personal salvation (John 3:16), spiritual and cognitive renewal (Romans 12:2) or a fellowship that is rooted in the reality of God. Moreover, any persecution that *Apple* fanatics face has more to do with not being able to access a certain app for their exclusivist *iPhones* than it does with being thrown to lions. Nevertheless, you get the idea. Yet, there is a more

---

[3] May he rest in peace.

potent point I wish to make which is somewhat apologetic in nature.

If there had never been an *Apple* computer built, logo designed, software written or advertisement bought do you think there would even be one *Apple Computers* fanatic in the world today? The answer is, no. The reason there are *Apple Computers* fanatics is that there really was a first *Apple* built. Moreover, followers of *Apple* have really had their lives changed, not by something subjective, but real. They really have witnessed the positive aspects of a paradigm-shift in the history of computers, music and phones. For this reason there are millions of *Apple*-ites in the world today. If the early church grew in a similar fashion during the same amount of time (30-35 years) why did it happen? I submit to you that it is because there really was a Jesus, who really did all the things that the gospels claim about him. He really did claim to be divine. He died on a cross, and rose again, in demonstration of those claims. That is why these first-century believers were willing to go to their deaths in unimaginable ways. They really had seen it with their own eyes.

If there is any question about this, 1 Corinthians 15:3-8

explains,

> For I delivered to you as of first importance what I also received, that Christ died for our sins according to the scriptures, and that he was buried, and that he was raised on the third day according to the scriptures, and that he appeared to more than five hundred brethren at one time, most of whom remain until now, but some have fallen asleep; then he appeared to James, then to all the apostles; and last of all, as to one untimely born, he appeared to me also.

Even atheist New Testament scholars recognize that 1 Corinthians was written by Paul in the 50s A.D., and that this passage contains a creedal statement that goes back even further than that. In another post perhaps I will take more time and show how it is that we can know people were claiming he was dead, buried and raised almost immediately after the events. The fact is, just as the rapid growth of *Apple Computers* demonstrates that there really is something going on here, so the rapid growth of the early church strongly counts in favor of the truth of the gospels.

It should be mentioned that I would never use this argument in a debate, or as a primary means of defending the faith. Nevertheless, I have always felt that the spread of the body of Christ in the first century, including the willingness of believers to die grueling deaths, is a powerful indication that they really believed in their claims. I realize other faiths (such as Islam) also spread quickly at their inception, but there exist striking differences. Just know that you have a legacy in the Christian faith that is rich and powerful. In fact, we should spread our faith with great passion - out of appreciation for those who died to deliver it to us. They are our spiritual ancestors.

Our old *Apple* from 2005 (which Sarah lovingly refers to as "Grandpa") is still kicking. Its cord has been held together by duct-tape and until we replaced the battery it would die if you looked at it funny, but it's hanging on. Yet, in the future *Apple* will surely disappear in the dust of some new company and operating system (how do I know? Call me an *Apple* doomsday prophet). I myself no longer use *Windows* or *Mac*, but *Ubuntu*. All human empires ultimately fall. This was a clear implication of Augustine's *City of God*. However, the church of Jesus Christ will remain forever.

(This website was created on a *Mac*)

IS HAPPINESS THE TRUTH: VICTORIA OSTEEN, PHARRELL WILLIAMS AND FREAKONOMICS

This year, we have been told that "happiness is the truth." Prosperity was once thought by westerners to be the highest level of fulfillment and the greatest goal of life - two cars in every garage and a chicken in every pot. Then the sentiment was reduced to what stands behind that desire for prosperity making it possible - money. However, scanning the documentary films on *Netflix*, popular books on *Amazon* and songs on *iTunes,* one comes to recognize that the reductionist evaluation has taken another culture-wide turn such that no longer is mere prosperity the goal, nor the money that stands behind it, but the happiness that all of these things are meant to bring. Happiness is now the highest goal of human endeavor. Like all engrained and evolving societal quirks this focus on happiness has permeated the walls of the church. When the culture coughs the church folk get the common cold.

Pharrell Williams released a huge track this year that can be heard, almost before you open your front door, blaring from car stereos, restaurant ambiance and product ads. The title? *Happy*. I like the song. I like Pharrell for his seemingly genuine humility about success. In fact, I don't just like songs about happiness. I like *being* happy. There have been moments when I have felt "like a room without a rough" whatever that means. What I don't like is the elevation of happiness to the highest goal of human endeavors. Beyond the harmless free spirited pop song, I don't like the idea that "happiness is the truth." Yet, this is what we are seeing. With this already on my mind, I selected a random podcast today and the sound of *freakonomics* materialized in my phone's speakers.

They were discussing whether religion can make people happy. Wrong question, but whatever. First they discussed tithing. Interviewing Southern Baptists at a church in Alabama and pulling together research data from those interested enough to look into the subject, they determined that tithers are generally happy people. However, the "non-religious" economist who became the primary authority on the matter, explained his findings that some folks tend to be less likely to attend services regularly if they are regular tithers. The assumption is that they slough off enough guilt by giving that they don't feel compelled to diligently attend. So the great advice that the non-Christian, non-churchgoing economist gave was that since one is the most fulfilled by actually attending the socially engaging worship services, he should *attend* more and *give* less. Problems abound.

Primarily, this is only good advice if happiness is the ultimate goal. Yet, this is why non-Christians have a hard time giving Christians advice on how to live out their faith. Happiness is not the ultimate goal, despite what the ever-popular wealth and prosperity preachers say. Truth is the goal. We should be searching for truth. Isn't that what the researchers are after anyway? If Christianity is true then it matters little what brings the most happiness - just ask Job, Jonah, Paul, the martyrs . . . you get the idea. Yet, in a world like ours happiness is the flowering rose of desire.

Victoria Osteen unintentionally awakened a sleeping giant

this week. Christians who understand the idolatry of happiness have assaulted her sermonette with great fervor. In case you missed it, she declared, *"I just want to encourage every one of us to realize when we obey God we're not doing it for God — I mean that's one way to look at it,"* she said from the pulpit. *"We're doing it for yourself, because God takes pleasure when were happy. That's the thing that gives him the greatest joy this morning ...just do good for your own self. Do good because God wants you to be happy."* The response from the crowd did remind me of a "room without a roof." Now I'm going to be one of only a few who give her the benefit of the doubt. Maybe she merely meant that doing what God wants you to do actually turns out to be the best thing for you anyway (although, that may not always be something that leads to happiness). Who knows? Yet, her comments demonstrate the longing for happiness.

I'm a Christian apologist who is well aware that the only serious atheist argument that resonates with folks is the argument from suffering. Often skeptics and Christians mistakenly come to believe that we exist for God to make us happy. Thus, when we get cancer, have heart problems, watch our children die or run out of money, we rail at God for failing us in some way. Emotional responses like this are to be expected. However, if we recognize that we were not merely made for God to make us happy then we still find him in the midst of our suffering. With the cultural belief that we are here for our own happiness we will be utterly bewildered in the face of such pain. See how dangerous this view is?

So, in the end, is it not the case that God does want what's best for his children, and will that not ultimately result in a state of happiness? Yes! That state, however, comes at the end of kingdom building and at the realization of the kingdom of heaven. Rather than happiness we get something more magnificent - joy. For now, what matters is the truth and it's not always happy.

Happy
Pharrell Williams

It might seem crazy what I'm about to say
Sunshine she's here, you can take a break
I'm a hot air balloon that could go to space
With the air, like I don't care baby by the way

Uh
Because I'm happy
Clap along if you feel like a room without a roof
Because I'm happy
Clap along if you feel like happiness is the truth
Because I'm happy
Clap along if you know what happiness is to you
Because I'm happy
Clap along if you feel like that's what you wanna do

Here come bad news talking this and that, yeah,
Well, give me all you got, and don't hold it back, yeah,
Well, I should probably warn you I'll be just fine, yeah,
No offense to you, don't waste your time
Here's why

Hey
Go
Uh
(Happy)
Bring me down
Can't nothing
Bring me down
My level's too high
Bring me down
Can't nothing
Bring me down
I said (let me tell you now)
Bring me down
Can't nothing
Bring me down
My level's too high
Bring me down
Can't nothing
Bring me down
I said

Hey
Go
Uh

Happy
Bring me down... can't nothing...
Bring me down... my level's too high...
Bring me down... can't nothing...
Bring me down, I said (let me tell you now)

Hey
C'mon

MY THOUGHTS ON HAVING ANOTHER GIRL

As we left the ultrasound room yesterday I encountered a strange cocktail of emotions. On the one hand, I realized that unless Sarah and I have another child (not likely), and unless that child is male (apparently less likely), my brother and his wife will have the last shot at continuing the family name. On the other hand WE'RE HAVING A BABY GIRL! So, you see my dilemma? I would have liked a boy, considering the extremely close relationship I have always shared with my father. Nevertheless, it was me who wanted a girl when we had Jolie. I have never been the stereotypical, "my boy is gonna be a quarterback," kind of guy. For that reason, I am genuinely excited about our new daughter. Furthermore, as I have considered this over the past 24 hours, I have surmised that girls are threatened by society in a unique way that makes the apologist in me humbled that God would give Sarah and I the responsibility of raising and defending the hearts and minds of these children.

Girls are being told that they do not need men

This really stinks for the boys of this generation. Guys know, deep down, that they need women. I know, I know. There is good biblical reason to believe that it is not God's intent for everyone to marry. Yet, men need women and women need men even outside of marriage. Men need a feminine perspective on matters of politics, culture, art, family and benevolence. Women need a masculine point of view as well. Whether we marry or not, God created them "male and female" for a reason. Unfortunately girls are repeatedly being told that they should be independent of men in work, family and everywhere else. Oh yes. One caveat to the last statement is in order. Its okay for a man to influence, instruct and even correct a woman if (and only if) he is a gay man. This has led to a skewed understanding on the part of many women with regard to their roles both socially and sexually.

Girls are praised for sexual independence

Because of all this, women are now encouraged to be dominant sexual creatures, and this has led to a serious problem which is not only unbiblical, but also seriously cripples a woman's chance at lasting happiness. Because women are being pressured (by other women) to engage in casual sexual encounters with random men (a la Sex in the City) they have become the perfect targets for predatory males who seek to use the woman's body for entertainment. This lessens the possibility that the woman in question will find herself with a man who wants to love, support and celebrate her for who she is. Ultimately, the woman who follows this culturally approved path will render herself the very sex object she denounces.

Girls are told that they can parent without a male

Because the female "independence" message has been pushed so far, women are now being told in countless movies, books and magazines that they can even raise children without the help of a man. The problem is that most woman in this situation become dependent on the state which is usually run by a male majority. No longer is the woman dependent on a single man (and he on her) who will love and care for her, but now she is dependent on a number of men who do not know or care for her. All of this is true without the mention of what unnecessary struggles the child will endure.

Girls are being told that the "Prov. 31 woman" is a self loathing housewife

Conversely, Scripture teaches that a woman has great value and that such value is often expressed by the way a woman speaks the truth about her God, raises and trains her children and loves and cares for her husband in a mutually dependent relationship. Such an image has become the target of an assault by many feminists in modern-day culture. In reality, the women who have made the biggest impact on me are the ones who fit firmly into the biblical framework. Moreover, I have discovered that the women who are the closest to God do not have a problem accepting a level of dependence. It has also been my pleased experience that these women are the most self-assured, confident (real confidence), content and happy people I know.

Unfortunately, the biblically minded woman is under attack

today. My desire for my girls is that they grow to be confident, educated, clear thinking, capable ladies who are able to accomplish whatever they set out to do. Yet, my desire is that they set out to do what God's will is for their lives. If they never marry I will celebrate that decision if it comes after prayer, Bible study and consideration. Nevertheless, I will unashamedly pray that God raises up wonderful theologically conservative Christian men for them to marry if that is how they find the Father leading them. Until that day I will defend their purity and biblically minded development tooth and nail. It is my goal that if the Hunter girls ever succumb to the deceptions of the culture milieu of their day it will not be because they were not trained in the truth by loving parents. I vow to be cautious of what they read, watch and hear, not in an attempt to insulate them, but so that when they have no choice in the matter they will stand firm in the truth.

THANK GOD FOR GIRLS!

AMBER-ALERT AT THE LOCAL STARBUCKS

NOTE: This post was originally made several years ago on my previous blog. Christopher Hitchens has since passed away of cancer.

Let's talk about coffee. If, by the title, you were expecting some sad human-interest story about an abused or abducted child then you came to the wrong place. I am going to tell you about a story of abuse and abduction, but not the kind of which you are thinking. First, however, I want to talk about coffee.

Do you remember the first time you ever bought yourself a cup? As a 90s adolescent, I was more fortunate than young men in previous generations in that straight, black, sugarless coffee was no longer what you had to regularly ingest in order to be inducted into the world of manhood. Cappuccino was en vogue, and if you really wanted to seem eccentric you could even order a latte. Times have changed. Now coffee is everywhere. You can even get "gourmet" caffeinated concoctions in the strangest places. What does this have to do with child abduction? Just hold on, I'm getting there.

People have become so obsessed with coffee that there are sometimes *Starbucks* shop's across the street from each other, as seen above. 21st century Americans spend hours at these places, (I earned my bachelors degree and wrote my first book at coffee shops). Furthermore, a lot of people are so obsessed with coffee that they not only spend time at *Starbucks*, but also have books about coffee, multiple coffee mugs, multiple coffee makers (espresso and regular), and even art to celebrate coffee. Perhaps they even have a god, as the mythical siren is featured in the center of the *Starbucks* logo. What does all of this have to do with child abduction? Alright, alright!

Christopher Hitchens is trying to destroy your child's faith in Christianity. You can brush this off and ignore the reality, but he has made the repeated claim that it is his desire that this generation of Christianity will be the last. He knows the Bible better than Jane and Joe Christian do (you'll recall from my previous posts that these are names I am using to represent average churchgoers). He knows church history better than Jane and Joe as well. He is a rhetorical master. By the way, he has compatriots in atheism at many institutions of higher learning where Jane and Joe's kid will go (I've met them). He has an army of like-minded teenage followers who regularly talk to Jane and Joe's kid at school, on the Internet and while playing *Xbox* (I've chatted with them). He is not tolerant of Jane and Joe's faith as they are his lack of it, and he is not harmless. His goal is to abduct Jane and Joe's kid into atheism. And they have no way of insulating their child from such influences. So now you might be asking, "What does this have to do with coffee?"

Do not stop reading after I make this statement. If Jane and Joe were as interested in an in-depth study of their faith as they are in coffee; they would know how to prepare their child for attacks such as these (Prov. 22:6). You might suppose that I am encouraging Jane and Joe to study their Bibles more. Yes, but also to study wonderful books that will help them develop (2 Tim. 2:15). By the way, I don't mean, the latest 5-minute devotional study. Rather, I am referring to books that scare you! Books you don't think you can understand are so rewarding when you finally do. Read books on theology, church history, and apologetics. Soften it up a bit with something from the Christian living section *if you must*. Jane and Joe cannot insulate their child, but they can equip him at home, using the knowledge they have gained, so that he will be prepared to stand on his own when attacks come. After all, it isn't just atheists like Christopher Hitchens who are after them, but false teachers within Christianity as well (Jude 1:4). Right now the Southern Baptist Convention is divided over a very important theological matter. Sadly Jane and Joe Christian would not even be aware of the subject. Now is the time to know what you believe.

At this very moment I am indulging in the most responsible addiction of the flesh. I'm drinking coffee. The good news is, I am about to continue drinking it as I study theology. Hitchens, the guy who is after your children, may sadly get his filthy hands on them and abduct them into faithlessness without their parent's preparation. However, I am going to do everything in my power to show my daughter that I am more interested in her spiritual growth than music, movies, food or caffeine. I will do all I can to prepare her, and I look forward to many long conversations about what God is doing in her life. Where will we have such talks? At *Starbucks*, of course.[4]

---

[4] Though Christopher Hitchens is now dead, there are a great number of atheists with his goals in mind. The sentiment of this article is more important than ever.

5 PRACTICAL WAYS TO GROW IN KNOWLEDGE FAST

It has become a common Christian refrain from our carved out subculture – "It doesn't matter if you know everything about God if you don't know God." Fair enough. The problem is that first, I've never met anyone who knows everything about God, and second, I know a lot of people who know him, but don't know much at all about him. Sometimes it's ok to say, "I need to learn more about the God I serve, and the world He created."

Almost ten years ago I became fascinated with Christian apologetics. I wanted to learn as much as I could as quickly as possible. In three months I went from knowing very little to being confident about teaching a class on the subject. The method I discovered can be used by anyone and with other categories than apologetics. I encourage all believers who desire to grow in knowledge to give it a try.

1. Listen to podcasts - Unless someone is with me I'm listening to some kind of educational audio almost all the time. This was a difficult switch because I love music. Even now, occasionally a new album will come out and I'll take a break for a few days, but for the most part if you see me driving I'm learning. The same goes for the gym.

From the moment I put on the ear buds and leave the locker room I'm listening to something. If you're into apologetics, my list includes *The Reasonable Faith* podcast, the *Defenders Class* (with William Lane Craig), The *Don Johnson Radio Show*, *Unbelievable* (with Justin Brierley), *Theology Matters* (with the Pellews), *Deeper Waters* (with Nick Peters), *The Dividing Line* (with James White - careful with this one) and of course, *The Trinity Crusades Radio Program* (with me and Johnathan Pritchett). To expedite apologetics learning, listen to debates. Listen to a ton of debates. This way you get to hear the defense and the critique. For a host of free resources check out *apologetics315.com*

If your not into apologetics (even though you should be) and you'd rather here sermons, check out *Let My People Think* (with Ravi Zacharias) or just pick any well known pastor. He's probably got a podcast. And if you're a pastor, and thus are expected to know everything about everything, you might enjoy *Stuff You Should Know*, *Stuff You Missed in History Class* and *Freakonomics Radio*. For a host of free seminary style lectures - check out *biblicaltraining.org*.

2. Listen to e-books on your phone - It's the 21st century and while you might be one of those, "I like to smell the pages" kind of people, the point is learning and you can learn a lot faster with modern technology. Most e-book software has a function to read out loud to you. You can even set it to double or triple speed (this is also true of podcasts). You have to work up to the faster settings and the computerized artificial voice is annoying at first, but you'll get there.

3. Use *Itunes U* and *Youtube* - Believe it or not *Apple* has made thousands of full courses from every imaginable institution of higher learning available for free. You can even get the study guides. Some of them are video related and some are just audio, but when I discovered this I got noticeably giddy. As far as *Youtube* is concerned, you have to be careful. Nevertheless, the site is good for everything from learning how to do laundry to understanding the cosmological argument for God's existence so don't discount it too quickly.

4. Talk to others about what you're learning - Do not skip this step! You need a learning buddy. It's best if you share enough interests in common with someone that you can talk about what you're learning together. However, any friend who is a good listener will do. Unless you have the greatest marriage in history, don't use your spouse. He/she does not want dinnertime to become a seminary lecture. Don't do it. Seriously. Don't.

I was fortunate enough that when I was first getting into apologetics my friend Andy was at about the same level of understanding. We read different books and then shared our insights with each other. This saved time by doubling the speed at which we were learning.

5. Pray - You will do none of this if you aren't passionate about the process. I recommend asking God to give you a passion for learning. He did for me. Then praise him for those truths.

DISTORTING DEFOE: HOW HOLLYWOOD SHIPWRECKED CRUSOE'S ONLY HOPE

I have since often observed, how incongruous and irrational the common temper of mankind is, especially of youth ... that they are not ashamed to sin, and yet are ashamed to repent; not ashamed of the action for which they ought justly to be esteemed fools, but are ashamed of the returning, which only can make them be esteemed wise men.[5]

The above quote is from the famous work, *Robinson Crusoe*, by Daniel Defoe. It comes early on in the story, just after Crusoe is a part of a shipwreck that very nearly results in the deaths of the entire crew. The captain warns him that the most appropriate thing for Crusoe to do is go home. God has given him a sign, he is told by the captain, and that any future life at sea will result in danger and calamity. At this our protagonist reflects with the above words.

---

[5] Defoe, Daniel, George Chalmers, and John Scott Keltie. *The Works of Daniel Defoe, Carefully Selected from the Most Authentic Sources. With Chalmers' Life of the Author, Annotated.* (Edinburgh: W.P. Nimmo, 1872) P. 39.

Thus, repentance becomes a theme, if not the primary theme, of the story. We hear of repentance again and again. This is because Crusoe has the great need to repent again and again as he ignores the captain's warning and is, consequently, abducted by pirates, on the run and finally shipwrecked on what at first appears to be a deserted island. Finally, he discovers a Bible and transforms from a nominal Christian into a relentlessly committed one. Upon rescuing his man Friday, a cannibal who is about to be cannibalized by an opposing tribe, he begins his first evangelistic work by leading the "savage" to faith in Christ. Beautiful! However, Hollywood got hold of the story and swiftly steered it into the rocks.

Upon finishing the book I thought it would be fun to check out the 1997 film adaptation starring Pierce Brosnan. Liberties must be taken, but this was just too much. In an attempt to inject romance, sexual references and at least one nude scene, the story is altered so that Crusoe embarks on his journey to flee his murder of another man that resulted from a love triangle. In the book, he was merely seeking adventure. This type of change, however, is to be expected from show business. The greatest offense has to do with the

Christian message. Once Friday is rescued by Crusoe they have a theological debate after which they decide that religion is one of the great vices of humanity, and Crusoe accepts Friday's culture. What? This turns the original story on its heels.

Christian faith is on every page of the book. Repentance is at its heart. God's providence in the worst of situations leads the primary character to muse,

> *How mercifully can our Creator treat His creatures, even in those conditions in which they seemed to be overwhelmed in destruction! How can He sweeten the bitterest providences, and give us cause to praise Him for dungeons and prisons! What a table was here spread for me in a wilderness where I saw nothing at first but to perish for hunger!*[6]

This transformation, of Friday and Crusoe, has led me to a renewed commitment to guard my daughters from the corruption of the thinking and philosophy that results from living in a culture which attempts to revise history and distort the true, the good and the beautiful. I do not want my daughters to be manipulated in reality the way the character of Friday has been in fiction. I hope that you will join me in that endeavor as it relates to those you may influence.

---

[6] Ibid. P. 78.

F18S, PREACHING AND THE DEFENSE OF THE FAITH

As I write this I'm on the east coast on Solomon's Island in Maryland. I've been speaking this week at Southern Calvert Baptist Church and it is one of the best evangelistic events I've ever been a part of in a church of this size. We have seen many saved and many commit to a closer walk with Christ. Yet, what I experienced yesterday spoke directly to me about preaching, evangelism and Christian apologetics.

Near here is the United States Naval Air Station at Patuxent River. On that base is the Naval Test Pilot School. The school trains elite pilots to actually do the testing on military aircraft. Only the best of the best are allowed to enter the school, and those who make the grade will have a heavy burden. Several astronauts were selected from the school including two men who are currently on our space station. There is no room for error. In the words of the Commanding Officer, they have to be both "geeks and warriors." They don't just know how to fly (everything), but they are also academically superior. They will also oversee the production of new technology that may or may not make it onto certain planes or helicopters. Each new piece of equipment must be shown to be of great value since space and weight on the control panels is limited. This, I think, speaks to the task of preaching, evangelism and Christian defense indirectly in several powerful ways. Namely, preachers and Christian apologists must:

1. Know how to "fly" - Simply put, preachers must know how to preach well. Every pilot that makes it to the test pilot school is already well trained and among the best in terms of his ability to manipulate his craft in the air. All the knowledge in the world will do the preacher no good in the goal of preaching if he cannot communicate his message in a way that connects with the people. There is a move among younger preachers, however, that certain types of preaching (the best in fact) involve ivory tower articulations of the passages they are preaching without illustration, humor, emotion or pathos. This kind of flying is bad. We need to actually connect. If we have all of the academics, but can't make our sermons "fly" then they will crash land on the audience. The same goes for any apologetic presentation.

2. Know their "equipment" - Preachers need to know their equipment as intimately as these pilots know theirs. There is an alternate movement among some pastors today that implies an understanding of the importance of knowing how to make their sermons "fly," but minimizes the importance of knowing how the "equipment" works. Both are necessary. This speaks to the Christian apologist as well. If those testing the equipment, that will serve in defense of our country, have to be incredibly knowledgeable about the minutia of their apparatuses - then we ministers certainly need to be at least as knowledgeable about the facts, biblical data and arguments used in the proclamation of the gospel and defense of that gospel. Though this will annoy some who don't see the value in such academics, the denial of this principle amounts to the affirmation that the defense of the US is more important than the defense of Christianity. I'm a patriot, but I serve a greater kingdom. If we are going to take the defense of our country that seriously, we need to take the defense of and preaching about our faith just as seriously.

3. Weigh the cost of new "technology" - Just as the "geek-warriors" at Patuxent River must get their new technology past waves of scrutiny before it is installed in military aircraft, preachers and apologists must do the same for every fact, argument, illustration, joke and biblical case they will involve in a sermon or presentation. Just as there is limited space on the control panel of an F-18, there is also limited space in any gospel presentation. Much material must be left on the cutting room floor. The CO at the test pilot school explained to me that often they develop or locate technology that they think will be an undeniable upgrade, but for whatever reason it is culled away. I can't tell you how many times I have personally been frustrated when writing a sermon, article or book and discovered that a piece of data or illustration that I was incredibly excited about just wasn't going to work the way I wanted it to for that particular project. The danger of just shoving it all in anyway should be obvious. On a military aircraft the controls will be confusing, the weight will be off, and the unnecessary gear will get in the way of a successful objective. For the Christian minister, the message will be confusing, the weight will be off (meaning that the presentation will go too long or drag the people down) and the unnecessary material will get in the way of the ultimate objective. Again, we need to take what we do as preachers of the gospel and Christian apologists at least as seriously as military personnel take the defense of our nation.

As I left Patuxent River I looked around at the various types of aircraft. They were all different sizes and served different purposes. One well-known jet had wings that were actually too short (a design flaw) making it hard to control. Even it served a great purpose in terms of training. They have helicopters that were in use during Vietnam. The CO explained that it's helpful to have older combat aircraft, because we can learn a lot from the designs of the past, even though they don't have all the bells and whistles of the newer models. You can easily see the other obvious analogies here with the differences in individual ministers' gifts and the value of the way aging veterans of the faith designed their own materials. In the end, though, I was inspired. I was impressed with the work being done at Patuxent River, but I was inspired by it to be a better preacher, evangelist and Christian apologist. I hope you will be too.

3 THINGS YOU HAVE TO REALIZE RIGHT NOW

The book of Esther reveals a situation in which God's people, the Jews, were in captivity in a comfortable place. After the Babylonians had conquered Judah and that holy City of Jerusalem they took God's people into bondage in Babylon and though they were in bondage they had a certain degree of freedom. They were allowed to live a normal life in this city, and what an incredible city it was. These captive Jews were brought in and carried past the gates of Ishtar bigger and more beautiful than any architectural achievement they had ever seen. The walls were 40 feet thick all the way around as the Babylonians boasted that they could ride four chariots side by side across the top. The city was full of bright colors and sounds (the blue bricks, for example, that made up the Ishtar gate were difficult to make. The color itself was unusual to find naturally in the Mesopotamian world). This place was amazing to the Jewish people who had never seen such sights. They would have continued along a road past the palace with walls even thicker than the walls of the city itself. In the inner most chambers of that palace was where Daniel prophesied. The Jews could see that they were going to have strong leadership. Then they would have seen the temple coming into view, four football fields large on bottom, 2 football fields large on the second level and one football field large on the top - high above the city where they would worship their gods while involved in drunken orgies. Sadly this would have been carnally enticing to many men. So by the time, years later, the Jews were set free, they had no reason to want to go back to Judah and the City of Jerusalem. They were quite happy and comfortable where they were.

1. Comfort is captivating - Francis Chan captured it perfectly when he said, *"But God doesn't call us to be comfortable. He calls us to trust Him so completely that we are unafraid to put ourselves in situations where we will be in trouble if He doesn't come* *through."*[7] Ultimately, Esther's risky explanation of her Jewish genealogy, combined with Haman's wicked plan to kill the Jews, and the king's timely case of insomnia all weave a tapestry of trouble for God's people and the way God, indeed, came through. That's what it took. The comfort had to go. The same is true for us.

Have you ever found yourself on your knees again pouring out your heart . . . again . . . to God for some sin . . . again . . . and feeling like he can no longer stomach your promises of change? I have. Part of the problem is that our sins are often comfortable. The chains have become more comfortable than crowns. Crowns can be so cumbersome. Chains can even be decorative. I don't mean to get too esoteric, but the point should be clear. It's very comfortable to use your smartphone to look at porn, your *Netflix* account to watch garbage, your little white lies to make yourself look better or your talent for telling good stories for gossip. We have learned to wear our Babylonian and Persian chains well. They suit us, we imagine. We are too lazy to learn a better fashion. We are comfortable.

---

[7] Chan, Francis. *Crazy Love*, (Colorado Springs: David C. Cook, 2008) P. 122.

2. Crusaders are called - *The Bachelor*, and similarly smutty reality shows, doesn't shock us anymore. But the story of the king and his search for a new bride (which involved a bunch of beautiful women being given makeovers and spending separate nights with him before being voted out of the mansion) was the original reality contest of this type. If television existed then, the talk of the town would have revolved around which beautiful girl was the favorite. When one of them got voted off, she would appear the next morning on *Good Morning Persia* and be interviewed by George Stephanopoulos on what life was like inside the palace walls.

However, God (though His name never appears in the book) had prepared two crusaders. Esther and Mordecai were in the right place for "such a time as this." The same is true for all believers. We must cast off our chains of comfort and recognize that we can no longer continue living like zombies, roaming the landscape intoxicated by carnality, but embody our call to be crusaders for God's plan. You are among people who need you, and they need to hear the message.

3. Condemnation is close - For the Jews in the story, Haman had convinced the King to order their genocide. The command could not be undone, but they were free to prepare themselves. As a result, the Jews won the day. The same is true for all humanity. Condemnation is close and while we cannot change that, we can prepare the world we live in by reaching others for Christ in the time we have left. If that phrase, "reaching others for Christ" sounds pat and cliché, the fact only speaks to the degree to which we have become comfortable with the denigration of conservative Christianity in our own Babylon or Persia. We are here for a purpose. We are here "for such a time as this!"

APOLOGETICS

CHRISTIAN DEFENSE IS OFTEN OVERLOOKED IN THE 21st CENTURY. NEVERTHELESS, THERE IS A RICH HISTORY OF WHAT WE CALL APOLOGETICS IN THE LIFE OF THE CHURCH. BELIEVERS SHOULD KNOW HOW TO ANSWER THE QUESTIONS OF GOD'S EXISTENCE, THE SOURCE OF MORALITY, THE SUBJECT OF OTHER RELIGIONS, BIBLICAL RELIABILITY, THE BEGINNING OF THE UNIVERSE AND MANY MORE THINGS. WHILE I HAVE WRITTEN SEVERAL OTHER BOOKS ON THIS ISSUE I HAVE TRIED TO MAKE THIS SECTION ACCESSIBLE TO CHRISTIANS WHO ARE NOT NECESSARILY ACADEMICALLY MINDED. AGAIN, FEEL FREE TO SKIP AROUND. IF A PARTICULAR ISSUE ISN'T ALL THAT INTERESTING TO YOU IT WON'T OFFEND ME. THESE ARE MY FAVORITE TRUTHBOMBS IN THE BOOK.

MOPEDS AND MORALITY: A REALLY SHORT STORY

"Today will be different," I think as my legs spill out of the bed and into the coziest of slippers. Half way to the kitchen I see that Rob ignored my mandate to clean his room yesterday. It's fine. I'm a new man. The disobedience looks different now. Passing the kitchen counter the program from last night's event creeps into view. "The End of Morality," is displayed in a stylistic font on the cover. I'm sold. The atheist convinced me. Morality is just a social development - a myth - a useful fiction. Nothing is objectively right or wrong. Today will be different. Today I will be the first skeptic to actually attempt to live a life consistent with the belief that there are no absolute moral standards. And hey, I'm proud of myself for not tearing into Rob over not cleaning his room. He did what he wanted, and while it may not be what I would prefer, it isn't wrong. It isn't right . . . it's nothing. One stiff cup of coffee later, I head for the shower and prepare for the day.

Grabbing the keys and heading for the door I shout to Cindy, "I'm taking off, sweetie!"

She answers with, "Sam . . . I meant to tell you . . . I won't be home until about 8:00 tonight! I have to stay late!" Stay late? Why would she need to stay late? More to the point, why has she needed to stay late so often lately? No matter. She can do what she wants, and I won't hold it against her. I'm a new man with a fresh outlook. She may not always choose to do what I'd like, she may do the opposite, but she's no worse for it. Nothing is right or wrong.

The drive to the office challenges my new worldview, but it's fine . . . it's fine. I wander two feet in my lane and the guy on the dumb moped flicks me off. Worse still, that's the same jerk I let cut in front of me at *Starbucks*. It's fine . . . it's fine. I've got to remind myself that justice is just an illusion anyway. Words like better or worse don't have any meaning either. Recalling last night's lecture I'm reminded that since there is no God, there is no objective or absolute grounding for morality. Words like better, worse, good, bad and progress have no meaning. Oh well. It's fine . . . the moped guy is fine . . .

Punching the power button on the car stereo I try to escape my annoyance by immersing my thoughts in the morning news. "Twenty dead in the middle east," the reporter announces. It's fine . . . it's fine. After all, wars have been waging forever. It's still a good idea . . . wait, can't use the word "good," . . . it's still the best . . . no . . . it's still the safest idea to eliminate the enemy.

Proud of myself I develop a lopsided grin and breathe, "See, Sam, it's not so hard to deny morality." No sooner do the words pass my lips than I hear the reporter explain the arrest of a local man who brutally raped and murdered a twelve-year-old girl who lived next door. "You gotta be kidding me," I say.

***

On the drive home I contemplate the day. Work was all right. I lost my promotion to Richard. Richard! Seriously? I almost confess that it isn't fair. But then, fairness has no meaning in my new worldview. If I'm honest, my resolve is weakening.

After the moped, the news reports and Richard's promotion I decide not to turn on the TV. I can't take any more. Perhaps, this is just the way it is when you try to look at the world in a different way. Maybe it isn't always going to be like this. I'll learn to control my emotions and see things the way they are. Everyone can do what they want. If people get hurt that's just the way life is. If I get hurt, I may not like it, but it isn't wrong . . . nothing is . . . wrong. I devour my reheated spaghetti in what must appear to be a disgusting manner, but I don't care. Besides, there isn't anyone here to see it. The meal is mediocre. Well, I can't use that word can I? Mediocre is a value statement. I'll just say, I'm not enjoying it very much.

Something creeps almost organically into my thoughts as I eat the tasteless noodles. Is Cindy having an affair? Speaking the word out loud I let it hang in the air almost as if I can see and examine it, "affair." Two hours pass and the word is still hanging there tauntingly in the same spot. Paranoia, jealously . . . whatever it is that holds the thought in place also drives me to my car and down the street.

In fifteen minutes I find myself at Cindy's office. As I drive it is as though all of the there's-no-morality self-help talk I'd been feeding myself all day falls away piecemeal with every passing mile.

Bursting into her office I see it. Is it . . . it can't be. It is. It's the moped guy. The word escapes my lips a second time, "affair." Again, it hangs there as my anger swells to a fever pitch. Cindy and moped-man begin trying to explain. Useless. I attempt to calm myself with the truth that what she has done, heck, what moped-man has done here is not wrong. Nothing is wrong. Then it happens. I realize the absurdity of what I had been telling myself all day. Of course it's wrong. It's extremely wrong. At the moment it reveals itself to be the most wrong thing that has ever happened to me. Morality is absolute, and this is absolutely immoral. End.

In those days there was no king in Israel; every man did what was right in his own eyes. - Judges 17:6

For when Gentiles who do not have the Law do instinctively the things of the Law, these, not having the Law, are a law to themselves, in that they show the work of the Law written in their hearts, their conscience bearing witness and their thoughts alternately accusing or else defending them, on the day when, according to my gospel, God will judge the secrets of men through

Christ Jesus. - Romans 2:14-16

THE MEANING OF LIFE

One agnostic voice that is suddenly getting a lot of attention is that of Neil deGrasse Tyson. He has now joined the ranks of Stephen Hawking and Bill Nye in bringing awareness of science (sprinkled with atheistic ideas) to the mass populace. Middle to upper-middleclass wanna-be elites can watch his programming and attend his live lectures and masquerade for an evening as progressive and academically minded lay-philosophers. Thus, it is not surprising that a video of one of Tyson's lectures is currently trending on youtube.com. Nor, is it surprising that it betrays his agnostic worldview. What is surprising is that it took a six-year-old boy to put his finger on the dilemma.

Then it happened -

When Young Jack asked Tyson the question, "What is the meaning of life," the audience oohed and awed. However, what most of the crowd was surely painfully unaware of was that this is one question thoughtful atheists and agnostics have a hard time with. After uttering all the essential condescending remarks on the cuteness of his questioner, Tyson answered,

> I think people ask that question on the assumption that meaning is something you can look for and then, "Oh I found it. This is where it is. I've been looking for it." Okay? And it doesn't consider the possibility that maybe meaning in life is something that you . . . create - you manufacture for yourself and for others. And so when I think of meaning in life I ask, "Have I learned something today that I didn't know yesterday, bringing me a little closer to knowing all that can be known in the universe. Just a little closer. However far away all the knowledge sits I'm a little closer. If I live a day and I don't know a little more than I did the day before, I think I wasted that day. So the people at the end of the school year who say, "The summer - I don't have to think anymore," I'm thinking, "what?" To learn is to become closer to nature. And to learn how things work gives you power to influence events - gives you power to help people who may need it - power to help yourselves - to shape a trajectory. So when I think of the meaning of life, to me that's not an eternal unanswerable question. To me, that is within arms reach of me everyday.[8]

Now this answer is the one most consistent with an agnostic/atheistic

---

[8] 6 year old Young Jack asks Neil deGrasse Tyson, "what's the meaning of life?" (http://youtu.be/BgMBGD6MZKc) Internet. Accessed on 25 January, 2015.

worldview. Though Tyson never explicitly says this (it would not sit well with his audience and would ruin the lovable moment), for the atheist there IS NO MEANING to life. There IS NO PURPOSE. One day all of humanity will be lost in some catastrophe or other and all of human achievement will disintegrate in the ashes of a pointless universe. It is for this reason that the cute little kid is asking the very question that I would also inevitably ask. The only difference is that I would press the issue further.

If there is no God true meaning and purpose do not exist -

For the reason I mentioned above, if there is no God or everlasting life then you can't assign meaning because, the term (in this context) loses all relevance. You can ask what the "meaning" of a phrase is, but ultimate meaning or purpose just doesn't and can't exist without God. In the absence of objective morality, value, solidarity, redemption or a future everything becomes as much a pointless waste of time as watching daytime television. In fact it's even less important than that. Tyson speaks of knowledge giving the individual a trajectory . . . Toward what? He says knowledge leads us to help others. Without God, why is that an objectively good thing? I'd merely be helping them get along a little more adequately until they are annihilated.

In the rest of the video he describes what people "should" therefore do. Says who? Without God, who's to say what I should or should not do? Without objective value and purpose, on what basis can he argue that one state of affairs is "better" or "worse?"

If there is no God you can't assign meaning or purpose to yourself -

Another problem with Tyson's recommendation is that even if there were purpose and meaning in the cosmos without God, you could never assign meaningful purpose to yourself. In order to have intrinsic meaning or purpose that is REAL a thing needs a designer. A hammer, for example, does not decide to be a hammer. Rather an inventor crafted neutral objects together and then declared the purpose of the new creation. It is a hammer. It is meant to put nail into boards. I am a preacher. In order for that purpose to be real I need an inventor. I needed someone to take some flesh and bone and determine that I would be used for the preaching of the gospel and the defense of the Christian faith. I have purpose for the same reason the hammer does. Namely, an inventor had a purpose in mind.

If there is a God he assigns purpose -

My daughter's favorite television show is *My Little Pony*. On one occasion a couple of years ago, she said, "Daddy, I know what I want to be when I grow up." With delight I waited to hear what my godly young offspring would aspire to do. She finished, "I want to be a pink pony." Now what should I say at that? Should I follow the societal drivel and affirm her with, "you can be anything you want to be and if you just believe hard enough, you can be that pink pony"? Of course not. The ontology is all wrong. She CAN'T be a pink pony. Moreover, there are a number of things that she technically COULD be, that MY daughter CAN'T be. For example she will also not work anywhere called *The Pink Pony*.

Yet, the reason I will not tell my daughter that she can be whatever she wants when she grows up is the same reason I will not tell her she can become an actual pink pony. That isn't what she was created to be. The inventor did not intend that purpose for her. Any purpose the inventor did not intend is not meaningful. To live out a self designated, made up purpose is to deny reality. It is meaningless.

So what do I tell my girls instead? Try to walk with God and determine what he wants you to become. Look for his purpose and meaning for your lives. After all, God is the inventor.

WASN'T THE NEW TESTAMENT JUST WRITTEN BY BIASED CHRISTIANS?

Should we really believe a book that was written thousands of years ago which talks about a man dying and then being raised from the dead? On the "debates page" of our website you will find where I have been challenged to give an answer more than once to this question. There is much that needs to be said in defense of the Bible that you can learn by exploring that part of our site. Here, however, I want to focus on what the New Testament is. After all, what the Bible claims about Jesus was recorded by Christians. In short, is it understandable for us to trust that they would be non-biased and give us the actual story? It seems like more people would be willing to take this stuff seriously if non-Christians had been the ones who wrote down the details of the death, burial and crucifixion.

First of all, to understand what the New Testament is, you

can't look at it as simply a religious book. Instead, you need to understand what scholars know; the New Testament is a group of the primary sources of the Christian faith. The Gospels, Pauline epistles and everything else, are the earliest (and eyewitness) documents of the life of Christ and rise of His church. It is reasonable to look to the Bible first because it is the oldest library of documents about Christianity.

But why do only Christians affirm the resurrection? I mean, if Jesus really rose again then why didn't non-Christians, at that time, write about it so we could get an outside perspective? The reason for this is that when people see that Christianity is true – they usually become Christians! Asking for an unbeliever's testimony about the resurrection is like asking someone who doesn't believe a car wreck just happened on Mulberry St. to describe the details of the wreck on Mulberry. If they saw the wreck, they are going to believe that it happened.

So, of course only Christians wrote the New Testament. We don't believe in it for no reason, but because it contains the primary sources of our Faith. For this reason, among many others, I am still understandably Christian!

TWO THINGS PRO-CHOICE ADVOCATES NEED TO HEAR

WARNING: I usually am not this direct, because I want to live up to the second half of 1 Peter 3:15 as a Christian apologist. However, this is an issue that warrants a little force. Please forgive my strong words and know that I only say this because I care.

Abortion is not a political issue, it's just an issue that has been politicized. What's more, the pro-life position is not one that can only be reasonably held on the basis of Bible verses. The separation of church and state mantra, which is given regularly by pro-choicers as a way of sidestepping the real discussion, is just a smoke screen. To make the point, here are two arguments (one mine, and one from Stephen Schwarz) that demonstrate that no thinking person (Christian or otherwise) should support the pro-choice movement. They demonstrate that abortion is a bad . . . nay . . . a bigoted, narrow-minded, backwoods, illogical, immoral, animalistic activity. See what you think.

First we have to understand one fact of which pro-choicers are painfully unaware. Among pro-choicers who are the most knowledgeable about this issue it is uncontroversial to admit that from the moment of conception there is new human life. Take the words of Peter Singer for example:

> It is possible to give "human being" a precise meaning. We can use it as equivalent to "member of the species Homo sapiens." Whether a being is a member of a given species is something that can be determined scientifically, by an examination of the nature of the chromosomes in the cells of living organisms. In this sense there is no doubt that from the first moments of its existence an embryo conceived from human sperm and eggs is a human being.[9]

In fact, Planned Parenthood use to be very straightforward about this. In a 1964 pamphlet discussing birth control, the group accidentally let the unborn cat out of the bag, saying, *"Absolutely not. An abortion ends the life of a baby after it has begun."*

---

[9] Singer, Peter, *Practical Ethics*, (2nd ed., Cambridge: Cambridge University Press, 1993) PP.85-86

healthy if they are born at least two years apart, rather than only a year apart. When babies are born two years or more apart, the mother has a chance to get back her strength before she has the next one. Furthermore, babies do cost money, and so more time between them gives the family budget a chance to recover, too.

WAYS TO PLAN YOUR CHILDREN

Birth control can help you plan your children so that you can have the number of babies you want and have them at times when you and your husband are well and able to take care of them. Birth control means the use of medically approved methods to postpone pregnancy until you are ready for it. The method your doctor advises for you is completely harmless.

Planning your children does not only mean being able to wait until you are well enough and able to take care of a baby. Family planning also means being able to have your baby when you do want it. Sometimes parents find that for natural reasons the mother does not become pregnant when the parents want a child. New discoveries in medicine give fresh hope to women or men who find they do not have children when they want them.

YOUR QUESTIONS ANSWERED

In order that you will have a better understanding of the means of family planning here are the answers to the questions which people most often ask:

What is birth control?

It is a safe and simple way to plan for your children and to have them when you want them.

Is it an operation?

It is not an operation of any kind.

Is it an abortion?

Definitely not. An abortion requires an operation. It kills the life of a baby after it has begun. It is dangerous to your life and health. It may make you sterile so that when you want a child you cannot have it. Birth control merely postpones the beginning of life.

Is birth control harmful?

As long as you have a doctor prescribe the method of birth control which suits you best, birth control cannot hurt you in any way.

Will it keep me from having a baby when we want another?

No. When you want another child, you simply stop using birth control. You

PLAN YOUR CHILDREN FOR HEALTH AND HAPPINESS

Images taken from LiveAction.org

Even the late great atheist, Christopher Hitchens (an atheist pro-lifer) explained, *"Unborn child seems to me to be a real concept. It's not a growth,"* he says, *"you can't say that the issue of rights don't come into question."*[10]

I'm no scientist, but here is the issue. Sperm cells represent male-human-biological-material, and eggs represent female-human-biological-material. When conception takes place the result is new-human-biological-material. In other words, new-human-life. If you are a pro-choice advocate and want to debate this issue then you need to hit the books (even thoughtful pro-choice propaganda material). This is not a controversial claim, but an accepted fact. The question is whether the living material has "personhood" or represents a new person. With this clarification, we are finally ready to consider two powerful arguments in favor of the pro-life position (and they are not religious arguments).

---

[10] Transcript – Hitchens, Christopher, (http://livingontheedge.org/broadcast/understanding-abortion-a-thoughtful-analysis-part-1/daily-radio#.VMVvfofxRSV) Internet. Accessed on 25, January 2015.

THE S-L-E-D ARGUMENT[11] - Stephen Schwarz put together what is in my opinion the best case against abortion that has ever been outlined for the masses. The word SLED is an acrostic. Those that are familiar with my ministry know that acrostics are my guilty pleasures.

S is for SIZE - If we are to determine that the unborn are not persons because of their sizes (i.e. they are only small collections of cells rather than full grown adults) then the argument of the pro-choicer proves too much. The claim would amount to saying that the smaller a human life is, the less it should be considered a person. Thus, short people are less whole persons than tall people. My wife would object to the notion that because she is head and shoulders less tall than I am, she is less of a complete person. I actually prefer petite women, so I would object on preference anyway. Yet, we all know that the size of a human life does not dictate the degree of personhood. We cannot bigotedly discriminate based on size.

L is for LEVEL OF DEVELOPMENT - A common pro-choice

---

[11] Steven Schwarz, *The Moral Question of Abortion* (Chicago: Loyola University Press, 1990), PP. 15-19

claim is that since the unborn are not just small, but "collections of cells" then they are not actually persons. In other words, they are less developed. They are not totally developed human life, but merely, potentially totally developed human life. The problem is that what can only be meant here is that the unborn are potential adult humans, but not yet adult (or fully developed). However, this again would prove far too much. My six-year-old daughter is also not a fully developed adult human. She is a potential adult human. Her level of development is at a reasonably early stage. Is she less of a person? Clearly not. In fact, my three-year-old daughter is even less developed than my six year old. The level of development has nothing to say about personhood. We cannot bigotedly discriminate based on level of development.

E is for ENVIRONMENT - The most used response in favor of abortion is that the unborn are not persons because of their environments. They are in the womb rather than outside of the womb. Because of this unusual location they are said to be potential persons, but not actual persons. The problem is that in no other aspect of life do we consider someone less of a person because of her location. Are Africans less persons in the eyes of North Americans because they are in a different environment? Does one's status of personhood change based on which room of a building they are inhabiting? Naturally, the answer is, "of course not." We cannot bigotedly discriminate based on environment.

D is for DEGREE OF DEPENDANCE - Since the unborn are dependent on the mother for survival (via nutrients, amniotic fluid etc.) the pro-choicers often imply that they are not persons and it is okay to terminate them at the will of the mother (who is, after all, supplying the means by which the unborn survive). But what about the disabled, the elderly inhabiting assisted living facilities, or anyone else who depends on others for survival? Do they also cease to be persons upon developing such needs? The answer is, no. They do not. We cannot bigotedly discriminate based on degree of dependence.

Thus, pro-lifers are justified in saying that abortion is not only wrong, but a bigoted, narrow-minded, backwoods, illogical, immoral, animalistic activity. At least, we would consider it to be all of those things upon applying the same logic to any other human life. Yet, I have another argument for the consideration of pro-choicers.

The Booth Argument - If one is still hesitant to agree that on the SLED case we should consider the unborn persons from the moment of conception, an argument in favor of erring on the side of caution should seal the deal. Imagine that before you stands a doorway, and in that doorway is a booth (like a phone booth, but with no windows). You want to pass through the doorway, but the booth is in your way. Perhaps you desperately need to get through the door, or conversely you may just wish to pass through the entry as a matter of convenience. Yet, you have no way of knowing whether or not the booth contains a person (in this case an adult man). The only way to pass through the doorway is to explode the booth, possibly killing its human contents if there is any. Now ask yourself whether you would be justified in going ahead and exploding the booth. At worst, you would be guilty of murder, and at best - reckless endangerment.

This comes to bear on abortion when one considers that at any stage of development the fetus may or may not have personhood. Naturally, a Christian will often contend that the fetus is definitely a person, but I'm framing this case for those who do not have those delimitations. If one does not accept the truth of Scripture, then the best they can do is say, "I don't know if the fetus has personhood at the moment of conception, but it might." Any attempt to argue that it certainly does NOT have personhood is merely based on an arbitrary belief. So the fetus becomes like the booth. The woman seeking to have an abortion can never say with certainty whether or not she is murdering a person, because she can never make an objective determination of whether or not the fetus is a person. Thus, if she "explodes the booth," she is guilty of murder (at worst) and reckless endangerment (at best). It is much safer to err on the side of life in such a case.

It is my hope that if you came to this article as a pro-lifer you will share it with others, and if you came as a pro-choicer you have seen that it's never a good idea to be a bigoted, narrow-minded, backwoods, illogical, immoral, animalistic, reckless person. After all, it's the 21st century. I thought the societal norm was to treat humans like humans. I thought the mantra of the day was, "I believe in science." Science is not your friend if you are a pro-choicer. Neither is philosophy. Neither is truth.

WHO MADE GOD?

Have you ever asked yourself, "If God made everything, then who made God?" If so, you're not alone. Not only do Christians ask this question, but also many skeptics point out that the idea of God makes no sense because he too seems to need a cause for why he exists. However, this is a misunderstanding not only about God, but also about the way the world is. Whether you believe in God or not, modern science has determined that when the universe began, time began as a part of the natural universe.

"Thus, physics predicts that time was indeed bounded in the past as Augustine claimed. It did not stretch back for all eternity. . . time did not always exist. . ."[12] That means that time is a part of what was made. It is a part of creation. Now since Christians believe that God created the universe, he stands outside, and is not a part of

---

[12] Davies, Paul, What Happened Before the Big Bang. (http://www.independent.co.uk/life-style/what-happened-before-the-big-bang-1584819.html) internet. Accessed on 24, January 2015.

it. After all, that's partly why he had to send Jesus into the world in order to save us from our sin. So if God stands outside of time then he, literally and scientifically, has no beginning and no end. Let's look at it formally.

1. Beginning and ending are words that have to do with time

2. Time is a part of the created universe

3. Things outside of the created universe are outside of time

4. Things outside of time have no beginning or ending

5. God is outside of the created universe because he created it, thus,

6. God has no beginning or ending

So if God has no beginning or ending then the question of who made God makes no sense. You might ask further, "Well, when did God come to exist?" This too is a senseless question since "when" is a term that indicates time as well. The best thing about this is that in spite of the fact that it is hard to get your mind around the idea of "no time," this lines up perfectly with modern science and the Bible. In other words, it makes sense. So the next time you wonder, "who made God," you'll have an answer.

GEEK GOD DENIES GOD: SCI-FI HERO STEPHEN HAWKING TRIES TO MAKE GOD "REDUNDANT"

WARNING: *This article gets a little more technical than the others, but with the release of Stephen Hawking's new book The Grand Design I felt that it was necessary. I also want to make it clear that I believe Hawking is a brilliant mind, and we have much to learn from him in many areas, but this does not mean we should take him to be speaking ex cathedra. This is particularly so when he talks about God.*

This week the world will encounter another tome by the eminent theoretical physicist Stephen Hawking. His 1988 work, *A Brief History of Time*, sold more than 9 million copies. Moreover, he has become a household name, even earning regular mentions on sitcoms, animated shows, and movies in addition to being cited in other popular and academic scientific works. His very publicized goal is to determine a "theory of everything" (TOE) which would explain special and general relativity. Naturally, he has much to say about cosmology. How did the universe get here? Why does something exist rather than nothing? Is there a beginning to the universe at all, or has it simply always existed? These are the types of questions that Hawking has attempted to answer in search of the TOE. In the past, it has been difficult for readers to determine whether or not there was room for God in Hawking's mind. Was he an atheist, deist, theist or still waiting patiently for the answer to the "God question" to be answered by his own research? Mathematician, John Lennox, has said of theoretical physicists such as Hawking, "They don't mind the idea of a TOE as long as God is not attached to it."

Regarding Hawking's new book, the quotes that have been released for publicity seem to indicate that Hawking may be trying to cash in on the renewed popularity of atheism. Yet, for all the talk of evidence for God's non-existence, so far it appears to be much ado about nothing. Granted, it's too early to make a determination about what Hawking says, since the book is yet to be released, but if the synopsis is correct, Hawking has not answered the objections that Christian apologists and fellow physicists have raised against his comments in the past.

Last year I was engaged in a written debate with the moderator of one of the internet's popular atheist websites. It was public and formal, though online. You can read it in full by clicking on the "debates" tab on BraxtonHunter.com.[13] Nevertheless, in this debate Stephen Hawking came up repeatedly as I set forth and defended a cosmological argument for the existence of God. However, I have supplied the comments related to Hawking and his views below so that you can become familiarized with the discussion.

BRAXTON: The universe exhibits incredible order. Stephen Hawking said in his book, *A Brief History of Time*, "It would be very difficult to explain why the universe should have begun in just this way, except as the act of a God who

---

[13] It is no longer featured on the website, but is an appendix to *CORE FACTS*.

intended to create beings like us."[14] Other scientists have said that it is like dozens of dials stand before us and if they were changed in the most infinitesimal way (if the gravitational force was slightly different or the strong nuclear force was changed or the electro-weak force) the universe would not be ordered as it is, but would result in chaos. This would seem to imply an intelligent designer.

WILL: Can you explain this quote from Hawking later in that very same chapter: "But if the universe is really completely self-contained, having no boundary or edge, it would have neither beginning nor end: it would simply be. What place, then, for a creator?"[15] Why does order imply an intelligent designer? Can you demonstrate that order cannot be without an intelligent designer?

BRAXTON: With regard to your question about the

---

[14] Hawking, Stephen. *A Brief History of Time: From the Big Bang to Black Holes*, (Toronto: Bantam, 1988) P. 126.

[15] Ibid.

eternality of the universe, yes I contend that it is a logically indefensible position to hold that the universe has always existed. In order for this to be so, time would have to stretch eternally into the past. However, if time stretched eternally into the past there would be an infinite number of points on that timeline stretching infinitely back. If there truly were an infinite number of points on that timeline, this point on that timeline, that we are inhabiting now, would have never arrived. This is why I said in my opening remarks that we would never have arrived at today. Stephen Hawking is a theoretical physicist. Thus, what he says about what the furniture (and form) of the universe might look like is to be taken as hypothetical. I mentioned him because he sees that if the universe has a beginning then it implies God. However, science is not in his corner on the hypothesis that the universe has no beginning or end. The simple philosophical demonstration I just mentioned above shows that there are no actual infinites in the universe. Moreover, Penzias and Wilson discovered the cosmic background radiation which demonstrates that the universe is in a state of expansion. If it is expanding then its expansion had to begin. Concerning the question of why order implies intelligence, I would first say that the burden of proof would fall on the side of naturalism to demonstrate an example of random variation resulting in anything remotely like the level of complexity we observe in the universe. Bill Gates claimed, "DNA is like a computer program, but far, far more advanced than any software we've ever created."[16] Beyond that, I would remind you of the points I made in my opening remarks.

WILL: I'm going to tackle the ordered part of this instead of your suggestion that Stephen Hawking is a theist.

BRAXTON: You never responded to my argument that an infinite regress is not possible. Rather, we heard an argument for the infinite universe. Steven Weinberg and Hawking himself admit that it is outdated. In fact Hawking claimed of

---

[16] Gates, *The Road Ahead,* (London, Penguin:, Revised, 1996), P. 228.

the background wave radiation that it was, "the final nail in the coffin of the steady state." By the way, I did not claim in my argument that Hawking was a theist. It is common in debate to use the very words of your opponents. My point was that Hawking admitted that if the universe was not infinite it would be hard to surmise anything other than a creator.

WILL: Hawking has said that the current incarnation of the universe is not infinite, but what has Professor Hawking said about the Cyclic model?

BRAXTON: Hawking's cyclical model (or any other of the many cyclical models) still does not solve the problem of the impossibility of an infinite regress so long as there are points (events, or points in time) on the timeline. The reason for this is that if there are points then there must be a first point.

After I said this, the discussion of Hawking did not continue in the debate. Yet, how does Hawking argue in his new book?

It would seem that Hawking replaces God as the first cause of the universe, in *The Grand Design,* with gravity. If gravity existed, Hawking seems to argue, then the universe would result. The problem with this is that the question then becomes, what caused gravity itself to come into existence. It would seem, so far, that Hawking's newest work will be a rehashing and repackaging of old attempts to remove God from the equation of the universe. Perhaps there will be new information and unique atheistic arguments, but truth will ultimately prevail and God's existence is certainly not in danger.[17]

---

[17] Everything I (and many other apologists) suspected about *The Grand Design* turned out to be true.

WHEN ORGANIZED RELIGION IS A PROBLEM: MUSLIMS AND METHODISTS IN BIBLE/KORAN COLLEGE TOGETHER

In a previous article entitled, *We didn't like church so we went to Walmart*, I mentioned that in America's most successful big-box store shoppers can exercise their contradictory lifestyle by picking up diet pills and workout equipment just a stone's throw from a full blown *McDonald's*. Well, the *Walmart* of seminaries is being born in the United States at *Claremont School of Theology*. In an article entitled *Interfaith U* (September 6, 2010) Elizabeth Dias writes,

> Four years ago, when the Rev. Jerry Campbell became president of California's renowned Claremont School of Theology, low enrollment and in-the-red books were threatening to close the 125-year-old institution. But since Claremont is the only United Methodist seminary west of Denver, Campbell resolved to find a way to keep it open. Drawing on classic American entrepreneurial spirit – when faced with extinction, innovate – and a commitment to engage today's multi-faith culture, Claremont this fall will

commence a first on U.S. soil: a "theological university" that will train future pastors, imams and rabbis under one roof." She goes on to say, ". . . they'll be helping tomorrow's religious leaders get a jump start on developing the wisdom and understanding needed to better guide a pluralistic society (emphasis mine)."[18]

I won't spend much time pointing out the brainlessness of this. Despite how theologically and philosophically ridiculous it is, we can all recall the eighth grade bully who exercised the Darwinian principles of his biology textbook by demonstrating that he was fittest to take our lunch money. Imagine how that bully might react if he was not only fit for the task, but also embraced a religious mandate to bully you in a more severe fashion. I know, I know. Claremont will no doubt train "peace-loving Muslims." And for those apologist friends of mine who deal with Islam on a regular basis, I am well aware of the differences in belief and emphasis from sect to sect. Nevertheless, the extreme-right-winger in me cannot help but point out a recipe for disaster when I see one. However, before moving on, it might interest readers to know that at least two other seminaries (*Andover Newton* & *Meadville Lombard*) have

---

[18] Dias, Elizabeth, Interfaith U, (http://content.time.com/time/magazine/article/0,9171,2013841,00.html) Internet. Accessed on 22, Janary, 2015.

followed the money-making strategy. We are certainly far removed from the crusades. At least that silver lining exists. However, we have gone to the other extreme. Yet, I would rather take this opportunity to speak to the question of organized religion. Is it a good thing or not? I believe in the local church, and though it doesn't sound politically correct, I believe in the organized church. Yet, when religion gets so organized that you can take a course on imam leadership in the same building as pastoral leadership there is a problem.

I am, at present witnessing to an atheist in my community. He is open, listening, and has admitted that at least one of the traditional arguments for God's existence has just about convinced him. Yet, he has expressed concerns regarding organized religion. We often hear the mantra, "I am a spiritual person, but I am opposed to organized religion." Slightly better is the confession, "I am a Christian, but opposed to organized religion." Many within the emergent church movement shouted such retorts for a short time. However, when the emergent church realized its own international conference circuits, best-selling books and mega churches it became hard to tout such an ideal. Nevertheless, our culture's emphasis on freedom and individuality has led many to embrace this way of thinking. It's happening in your community. A friend explained a dilemma he is having in his own ministry in which a family is pushing for the self-explanatory "home-church movement." Is there any good reason to embrace this model?

If we placed the claims of the organized religion opponent (ORO for short) into a logical formula we might state it in several ways. If they are opposed to it because it engenders corruption on the part of ministers then the argument might look like this:

1) I am against corruption,

2) Organized religion can lead to corruption, so

3) I am an ORO.

The problem with this is that it would also rope the ORO into opposing any form of government, law enforcement, business and even the family unit. The same could be said if you replaced the word corruption with any of the other claims that are made in opposition to organized religion by the ORO. The one exception may be the claim that religion is a personal thing and shouldn't be practiced or discussed in public. However, this claim would not be made by a Christian who has any depth of knowledge about his faith. The great commission (Matt. 28:16-20) mandates that Christianity be spread and shared openly. As my pastor friend pointed out, "With all its flaws, the local organized church is still the greatest force for good, evangelism and missions in the world today." It should also be mentioned that without the organized movement of God there is no reason to believe that any present-day Christian would have ever heard the truth, or professed Christ. Thus, it is exceedingly ungrateful to speak ill of the organized effort that carried the salvific message to our doorsteps.

I guess this means that I am in favor of organized Christianity, but not the organizing of Islam, Mormonism, Hinduism, or any other false religion. Furthermore, I couldn't be more opposed to the style of organized religion we see taking place at *Claremont* and other schools. It somewhat reminds me of the way competing fast-food restaurants have begun functioning under one roof, and even using the same employees. And as silly as the thought of diet-pills sitting on a shelf in view of a McDonald's franchise may be, it does not approach the collision of worldviews which will take place this fall in our *"One Nation Under God."*

4 REASONS SCIENCE IS NOT AT ODDS WITH RELIGION

NOTE: While the Bill Nye vs. Ken Ham debate specifically focused on the truth or falsity of evolution and creationism, this post addresses the bigger question of the relationship between science and religion.

Several weeks ago a highly publicized debate took place between evolutionist, Bill Nye and young-earth creationist, Ken Ham. Now while there is a wide range of opinions held by evangelical Christians with respect to Ham's understanding of Genesis 1-11, how he performed in the debate and whether a debate of this kind should be had at all, a tired old question has resurfaced. What is the interface of science and religion? Specifically, from this debate we are asked to consider whether Bible-believing Christians are even capable of doing good science without checking their Christianity at the door. They can for at least four reasons.

1. Christianity affirms scientific discovery

Biblical passages such as Psalm 111:2 describe the wonder that man has upon discovering the beauty with which God has created the natural world. For centuries, Christians have devoted themselves to scientific undertakings precisely because they saw science as a way of understanding their creator in a greater sense. Believers have founded institutions of higher learning, established hospitals and contributed to the scholarly community in undeniable ways. The notion that science is somehow at odds with the Christian message is absurd.

2. Science is not the property of atheism

Nor, does it count in favor of atheism. Listen to the archives of the *Don Johnson Radio Show*[19] and you will discover that often when a skeptic is asked to produce a piece of data that counts in favor of atheism and is opposed to Christianity they will (with glib certainty) say, "science." The idea was repeated liberally in the Nye-

---

[19] You may recall that Don endorsed my book, *CORE FACTS*. His podcast is outstanding and I recommend it to everyone.

Ham debate. What the atheist/agnostic means to say is that science works. It is incredibly efficient for studying the natural world. Yet, here there is a gross leap in logic to the idea that all that exists is the natural world.

Just because there is a natural world, and science does a good job studying it, does not mean that there is not a supernatural world (or supernatural aspects of the natural world). In other words, Christians agree that science is a great tool for doing an investigation of the natural world. Thus, the effectiveness of science doesn't count as a point in favor or atheism. It is something that atheists and Christians agree upon.

A popular analogy in use by Christian defenders involves the effectiveness of metal-detectors at locating metal. Metal-detectors are great tools. However, if one had the best metal-detector in the world it would not mean that because that device was so good at locating metal that rocks and trees and wood must not exist also. Science is great at what it does, but this no more means that the natural world is all that exists than the great metal-detector means that metal is all that exists.

3. Many scientists are Christians

I would have done several things differently if I were debating Bill Nye, but there was at least one thing Ken Ham presented that I thought was spot-on. We were treated to a video presentation of several accomplished scientists that were also Christians. If the question is whether or not certain Christian beliefs hinder the progress of science, this should count strongly in favor of the Christian position. Moreover, whether Ham's testimonials were cherry-picked or not, the idea that there are very few professional scientists who are religious is demonstrably false. Below is an excerpt from a recent book chronicling the research into this very question:

> The public's view that science and religion can't work in collaboration is a misconception that stunts progress, according to a new survey of more than 10,000 Americans, scientists and evangelical Protestants. The study by Rice University also found that scientists and the general public are surprisingly similar in their religious practices. The study, "Religious Understandings of Science (RUS)," was conducted by sociologist Elaine Howard Ecklund and presented today in Chicago during the annual American Association for the Advancement of Science (AAAS) conference. Ecklund is the Autrey Professor of Sociology and director of Rice's Religion and Public Life Program. "We found that nearly 50 percent of evangelicals believe that

science and religion can work together and support one another," Ecklund said. "That's in contrast to the fact that only 38 percent of Americans feel that science and religion can work in collaboration." The study also found that 18 percent of scientists attended weekly religious services, compared with 20 percent of the general U.S. population; 15 percent consider themselves very religious (versus 19 percent of the general U.S. population); 13.5 percent read religious texts weekly (compared with 17 percent of the U.S. population); and 19 percent pray several times a day (versus 26 percent of the U.S. population). RUS is the largest study of American views on religion and science.[20]

Simply put, there is little difference between average Americans and professional scientists when it comes to the percentage who are "religious."

4. The scientific methodology isn't necessarily different

Methodological naturalism has to do with the assumption a scientist (or anyone else) must make when doing a scientific investigation that the explanation of a given natural fact or phenomenon is a natural (not a supernatural) one. In other words, atheistic scientists and Christians who are scientists alike will be unlikely to assume that a supernatural explanation for the

[20] Ruth, David, (Misconceptions of Science and Religion Found in New Study. http://news.rice.edu/2014/02/16/misconceptions-of-science-and-religion-found-in-new-study/) Internet. Accessed on 22 January, 2015.

development of sea-foam, for example, is better than a natural one. But metaphysical naturalism is quite different. This is the view that the natural world *is* all there is. Clearly, a Christian has no problem with methodological naturalism. And, thus, can happily do science along-side his atheist colleague.

I say all of this for two reasons. First, I fear that there is an unconscious defensiveness on the parts of many Christians when it comes to science because they have unknowingly adopted the false impression that science and faith are at odds. They are not. If Christianity is true then *true facts* about the natural world will not contradict the Christian message. Like our forbearers, Christians should confidently approach science with enthusiasm and interest. Second, the conflict really exists between Christian values and worldly values, Christian philosophy and false worldly philosophies, political views that spring forth from a Christian worldview and political ideas that arise from non-Christian worldviews. Can non-Christian scientists be guided by their personal philosophies and produce biased conclusions? Certainly! And when this happens Christians should be prepared to point it out. For this very reason, I pray that God will raise up a generation of professional Christian scientists who are enthusiastic about the truth.

5 REASONS THINKING CHRISTIANS DON'T AFFIRM OPPOSING WORLD VIEWS

I have written this brief article for Christians to share with other Christians or with skeptical friends when faced with the question of why evangelicals speak as though their own worldview represents the only true religion. If you are reading this then perhaps it is because some believer passed it along. I simply ask you to consider these thoughts in an open-minded way. In fact, I'm not even presenting an argument for the truth of the Christian message. This is simply an explanation of why your believing friends cannot allow the claims that all religions are valid, or that religious beliefs are personal and beyond criticism to go unchallenged.

1. Objective religious propositions are either true or false

One of the major problems with the idea that Christians are just being narrow-minded, elitist and bigoted is that faith should not be an issue of personal preference or cultural heredity. Thinking Christians believe the message because they think it happens to be true. There is an unconscious belief, in the western world, that religious or spiritual claims are not true or false in the same sense that other things are true or false. The undeniable implication of this mistaken idea is that religious beliefs are not as real, important or urgent as others.

2. If Christianity is true then worldviews that oppose its claims are false -

For example, unless one is a cognitive relativist, they will not quibble with the claim that Barack Obama was president of the United States of America in 2014. The statement can be accepted as true. Likewise, the statement that Lady GaGa was president of the US in 2014 can be deemed false. What thinking people should recognize is that the claim, Jesus rose bodily from the dead as Scripture says, or that he truly said (and was correct) that "No man can come to the Father but by . . ." Jesus, is also true or false in the same way. In other words, objective religious propositions are either true or false just like any other objective truth claim. Thus, if Jesus is truly God incarnate, then Islam's claim that he was one of the greatest prophets, but not God incarnate - is false. If it is true that Jesus died by Roman crucifixion (as even skeptical historians accept) then Islam's claim that "he did not die, they did not crucify him" is false. This holds true for any opposing world view, and it should be said that any world view that is not an orthodox Christian world view is an opposing worldview to Christianity. In short, Christianity is either false and some other world view true, or Christianity is true and all opposing world views false, but they are not all true - nor are they beyond being true or false.

3. The truth of Christianity is too important to water down for the sake of unity with opposing worldviews -

Because religious propositions are either true or false if Christianity has true propositions about the nature of the afterlife, a God who loves and wants to commune with his creation or the means by which one can attain everlasting life and avoid everlasting separation from God then it is urgent. It is not merely too important to water down. It is more important than any other issue one will consider in reality. While not wishing to sound cold to anyone suffering in these areas, it is more important than financial difficulty, medical concerns, political movements, war or anything else. If this sounds controversial to you, it shouldn't. You can disagree with whether or not Christianity's claims are true in fact, but you cannot rationally argue with the statement that if they are true they speak to the most central and urgent problems man will ever face. This becomes all the more potent when we consider that the central message cannot be knitted together with the views of other religions. As Oxford and Regent College Professor, Alister McGrath explains, "Christianity has a particular understanding of the nature, grounds, and means of obtaining salvation."[21] He further explains, "The Christian tradition bears witness to a particular understanding of God and cannot be merged into the various concepts of divinity found in other religions."[22] This is why your Christian friends treat the issue as vital. It is also the reason why, though they shouldn't, they may

---

[21] Hick, John, Dennis L. Okholm, and Timothy R. Phillips. *Four Views on Salvation in a Pluralistic World.* (Grand Rapids, MI: Zondervan Pub. House, 1996) Pg. 174.

[22] Ibid. P. 165

even go too far and speak in hurtful or forceful ways about your unbelief. It's not that they think they are better or brighter, but because they know that you undervalue the importance of this urgent matter.

4. Religious views are not valid just because they are personal or represent a different perspective -

I agree with the world's most famous atheist, Richard Dawkins, on at least one thing. Religion is not immune to criticism just because it is personal. In his famous book, *The God Delusion*, Dawkins explains,

> As long as we accept the principle that religious faith must be respected simply because it is religious faith, it is hard to withhold respect from the faith of Osama bin Laden and the suicide bombers. The alternative, one so transparent that it should need no urging, is to abandon the principle of automatic respect for religious faith.[23]

A religion or worldview is valid if it is true. If it is not true then it should not be believed. If Christianity is true and Hinduism,

---

[23] Dawkins, Richard. *The God Delusion*. (Boston: Houghton Mifflin, 2006) Pg. 345.

Islam, the message of the Kingdom Hall of Jehovah's Witnesses, Mormonism, Scientology, atheism and all other worldviews are false, then people should be Christians. They shouldn't be Christians only because they were raised that way or it makes them feel good about themselves. Nor should anyone believe anything else for such trivial reasons. We should believe what happens to be true.

5. Most worldviews contain truths about the nature of reality and theology, but this does not mean that the religion itself is true -

I accept the methodological naturalism that atheists and Christians share when doing science - I reject the metaphysical naturalism which says the physical universe is all there is, was or ever will be. I accept the Mormon belief that we should trust inspired Scripture - I reject the documents they consider to be inspired Scripture aside from the Bible (and I reject how they understand the Bible itself). I accept the Muslim belief that there is one God - I reject their understanding of what God is like. I accept the Muslim belief that Jesus is a prophet - I reject the notion that he is not also priest and king. The point is that while I cannot say that these or other religions are "entirely" false (they do have some truth in them), I can say that if Christianity is true those worldviews themselves are false.

The bottom line is that Christians think religions and worldviews actually matter because they are making claims about reality. Most reasonable non-Christians will agree that we should believe things not because we like them, but because they are true. We are seekers of truth and want to share that truth with others.

HOW MANY ATHEISTS DOES IT TAKE TO PUT UP A BILLBOARD

The latest atheist attention grab is taking place in the south. Billboards will be placed in Nashville and Memphis, Tennessee, St. Louis, Missouri and Fort Smith, Arkansas with a picture of a girl writing her annual letter to Santa Claus pleading, "Dear Santa, All I want for Christmas is to Skip Church! I'm too old for fairytales." In an article about the stunt, David Silverman is quoted as saying, "Today's adults have no obligation to pretend to believe the lies their parents believed. It's OK to admit that your parents were wrong about God, and it's definitely OK to tell your children the truth."[24]

Despite the presumptuous implication that southerners need

---

[24] Foster, Peter, American Atheists launch provocative campaign in religious Deep South, (http://www.telegraph.co.uk/news/worldnews/northamerica/usa/11265926/American-Atheists-launch-provocative-campaign-in-religious-Deep-South.html) Internet. Accessed on 25 January, 2015.

Silverman and co. to tell them what they are and are not obliged to do with respect to the God debate, the group seems to have no problem implying that we *are* obliged to give a strong voice to *atheism*. When responding to the fact that no one owning advertising space in Jackson, Mississippi was willing to work with their organization they complained, "The fact that billboard companies would turn away business because they are so concerned about the reaction by the community shows just how much education and activism on behalf of atheists is needed in the South."[25]

The article speaks of the rise of atheism in America, but is this rise as dramatic as we're being told? According to *Pew Research* data, "2.4% of American adults say they are atheists when asked about their religious identity." The problem with this is that a lot of them don't know what the term even means since the same study showed that,

> Although the literal definition of "atheist" is "a person who believes that God does not exist," according to the Merriam-Webster dictionary, 14% of those who call themselves atheists also say they believe in God or a universal spirit. That includes 5% who say they are 'absolutely certain' about

---

[25] Ibid.

the existence of God or a universal spirit. (emphasis mine). [26]

So the actual number of atheists, despite what some people call themselves, is less than 2.4 percent. Also consider that "38 percent are ages 18-29"[27] and the lower half of that demographic may or may not remain in the atheist camp. In short, they make up a small, but very vocal minority.

Nevertheless, the representation of that minority in pop-culture is astonishing. Whenever we see them portrayed in fictional television or movies, atheists are hip, smart, witty, attractive and always win the "argument." Meanwhile, the Christian is often depicted as the uneducated redneck with one tooth in her head. Such is the case in the famous "atheist clip" from the *Netflix* original *Orange is the New Black* (I do not recommend watching this clip - I only mentioned it as evidence).

My advice, for what it's worth, is for Christians to be aware of the fact that these sorts of drive-by cultural prompts are more powerful than lectures from atheist professors and we should take

---

[26] Lipka, Michael, 5 Facts About Atheists, (http://www.pewresearch.org/fact-tank/2013/10/23/5-facts-about-atheists/) Internet. Accessed on 25 January, 2015.

[27] Ibid.

them seriously. However, we should not play into the mistaken belief that atheists are falling out of every window. Nevertheless, atheists have become "evangelistic" for their cause. Of the New Atheist movement, Scott Stephens writes,

> By comparison, the "New Atheists" look like sensationalist media-pimps: smugly self-assured, profligate, unphilosophical and brazenly ahistorical, whose immense popularity says rather more about the illiteracy and moral impoverishment of Western audiences than it does about the relative merits of their arguments.[28]

And in that sensationalist way, they are running an ambitious outreach program that is aimed at this generation.

In closing, since the article references the secularization of the UK, here is one of my favorite quotes from William Lane Craig on atheism across the pond:

> I wonder if something culturally significant is going on here. Several years ago, I asked the Warden at Tyndale House in Cambridge why it is that British society is so secular when Britain has such a rich legacy of great Christian scholars. He replied, "Oh, Christianity is not underrepresented among the intelligentsia. It's the working classes which are so secular."

[28] Stephens, Scott, The Poverty of the New Atheism, (http://www.abc.net.au/religion/articles/2011/01/19/3116506.htm) Internet. Accessed on 25 January, 2015.

He explained that these folks are never exposed to Christian scholarship because of their lack of education. As a result there is a sort of pervasive, uninformed, village atheism among them. I wonder if something like this could be happening in the States. I was surprised to see the number of blue collar folks from the community buying Harris' book and thanking him for all he has done. They didn't seem to have any inkling that his views had just been systematically exposed as logically incoherent. The intelligentsia have almost universally panned Harris' recent book (read the reviews!). Yet it is lapped up in popular culture. Wouldn't it be amazing if unbelief became the possession mainly of the uneducated?[29]

---

[29] Craig, William Lane as quoted in the article, The Eve of Village Atheism, (http://talithakoumfiles.blogspot.com/2011/04/eve-of-village-atheism.html) Internet. Accessed on 25 January, 2015.

THEOLOGY

THE MATERIAL IN THIS SECTION IS INTENDED TO ASSIST BELIEVERS IN UNDERSTANDING THE THEOLOGICAL CONCEPTS OF THE BIBLE. YET, NOT ONLY DOES IT COVER WHAT GOD IS LIKE, IT ALSO TOUCHES ON THE NATURE OF OTHER SUPERNATURAL BEINGS, SALVATION, MIRACLES, HELL, SACRIFICES AND OTHER THINGS. IT IS NOT ENOUGH TO KNOW WHY YOU BELIEVE WHAT YOU BELIEVE. WE ALSO NEED A GENERATION OF CHRISTIANS WHO KNOW WHAT THEY BELIEVE. INGEST THIS SECTION WITH ENTHUSIASM AS YOU LEARN TO ANSWER SOME OF THE TOUGHEST MATERIAL THAT GOD'S WORD TOUCHES UPON. AS I HAVE SAID IN OTHER SECTIONS, MOST OF THIS IS STILL UP ON MY MINISTRY WEBSITE. I WOULD LOVE TO HEAR YOUR THOUGHTS AND COMMENTS THERE. WHAT TRUTHBOMBS DO YOU HAVE?

3 VIEWS ON HELL

Hell is one of the most horrifying concepts in the Bible. For most of the 20th century there was little question among the people in the pews as to what the Bible taught on this tough subject. You don't want to go to hell because you don't want to experience everlasting fire. Oh, by the way, there's brimstone too. Let me tell you, as a child I had no idea what brimstone was, but it was still a torturously frightening word. And then as an afterthought you won't be with Jesus. There is, though, a renewed debate over this issue and it's time to define the positions for the layman.

Traditionalists - Most common among mainline evangelicals is the idea that man will experience eternal conscious torment in hell. For that reason, many have come to refer to this view as the ECT position. The traditionalist or ECT position holds that all who die without Christ will ultimately endure an everlasting existence of pain and suffering in which they not only exist, but are also aware of what is happening. This springs forth from passages like Mark 9:43 & 44 which says,

> *If your hand causes you to stumble, cut it off; it is better for you to enter life crippled, than, having your two hands, to go into hell, into the unquenchable fire, where their worm does not die, and the fire is not quenched.*

Those familiar with the passage know that it goes on to similarly describe how one should cast off two other body parts if need be to avoid going to hell. Each time, the refrain appears again, "Where their worm does not die, and the fire is not quenched." One would be right to assume that Jesus wants everyone to be clear about that point. Taking Jesus at face value, the majority of the church (for centuries), has believed that hell is an everlasting existence in which one will never be free from some sort of conscious suffering. Nevertheless, within traditionalism there is some latitude.

Some traditionalists believe that while one should take this passage, and others like it, to mean that hell will be a place of eternal conscious torment, one should not interpret the flames themselves to be literal. After all, the word translated "hell" here is the word "Gehenna" and refers to an actual geographical location outside the walls of Jerusalem. It is not the focus of this article to explain the history of the Valley of Hinnom, but it will do to simply say that it was a garbage dump to which Jesus pointed as illustrative of the separation we have come to call "hell." Advocates of the metaphorical traditionalist view will argue that, for this reason, the burning (of garbage perhaps) should not be taken to indicate that the actual existence of an unbeliever in hell will involve this sort of literal fire. Furthermore, this sort of apocalyptic imagery might involve trappings like this that are meant to point to a reality far worse than the image given. Nevertheless, those in this camp still affirm that those in hell will experience eternal conscious torment, but it will simply be a different type of torment.

Conditionalists - The conditionalist view says that the soul, like the body, is not innately immortal. That is, one's soul will not exist and live for all eternity unless God grants immortality to an individual's soul that he will only do in the event that one becomes a believer. In other words, immortality is conditional. This is why conditionalism is paired with what is called annihilationism. On the conditionalist/annihilationist view, those who go to hell will suffer for a period of time (or not - this is something annihilationists are divided about) before being annihilated (or ceasing to exist). Such a state can be called everlasting death, since the person in hell will remain dead everlastingly (that is to say, he won't be resurrected). He is not conscious. He does not feel. He is, body and soul, dead. This view is based upon passages like Matthew 10:28. This passage flatly explains, "*Do not fear those who kill the body but are unable to kill the soul; but rather fear Him who is able to destroy both soul and body in hell.*" We understand the killing of the body to entail what we commonly think of as physical death, and this passage includes the death of the soul in the same context. Little comment is needed to see why annihilationists understand Psalm 37:38 to support their view. It says, "*But transgressors will be altogether destroyed; The posterity of the wicked will be cut off.*" Therefore, says the annihilationist, the soul will ultimately meet its end, as will the body.

Now, in fairness, the gut reaction might be to think that these proponents reject the authority of Scripture, or are driven merely by emotion. To this, John Stott explains,

> I am hesitant to have written these things, partly because I have a great respect for longstanding tradition which claims to be a true interpretation of Scripture [eternal punishment in hell], and do not lightly set it aside, and partly because the unity of the worldwide Evangelical constituency has always meant much to me . . . I do plead for frank dialogue among Evangelicals on the basis of Scripture. I also believe that the ultimate annihilation of the wicked should at least be accepted as a legitimate, biblically founded alternative to their eternal conscious torment[30]

Universalists - The universalist takes a different approach altogether. While some universalists have aligned with unitarians (who deny the Trinity) many simply argue that either (1) there is no hell, or (2) hell is a place of reformation for sinners before they are allowed into the presence of God. This is partly because they see the love of God overpowering his wrath, anger and justice. Scripturally, though, they understand passages that speak to universal atonement (1 Timothy 2:6, 1 John 2:2 etc.) as implying that every individual not only can be saved, but will be saved.

---

[30] Edwards, David L., and John R. W. Stott. *Evangelical Essentials: A Liberal-evangelical Dialogue* (Downers Grove, IL: InterVarsity, 1989) p. 319-20.

Now, I find it difficult personally to imagine that, in the case of the universalist, the early church martyrs would have been willing to die such grisly deaths knowing that all men would ultimately be saved regardless. With respect to the conditionalist, I remain unconvinced. The biblical data regarding the horror and everlasting nature of hell still leads me to believe that it is referring to eternal conscious torment. Nevertheless, these are issues that are now rising to the surface in the evangelical church, and conservative traditionalists need to know what their opponents are saying.

MIRACLES

This article on the subject of miracles is the first in a new blog series that will continue indefinitely. Often times Christianity is said to be strange, outlandish, superstitious and just plain weird. If God can do anything, then Why did Jesus have to die on the cross? Isn't the idea of the Trinity just silly and impossible? Are we really supposed to believe in miracles when we live in such an advanced 21st century world? I plan on answering all of these questions to the best of my ability through these new posts in a grand experiment to show that Christianity isn't weird (something that many Christians won't admit), and that it actually makes perfect logical sense. I am also trying to make this as simple and accessible as I can so that you'll actually read, and recommend it to others. However, first things first, let's talk about why miracles aren't weird.

We begin with miracles because if one rejects their

possibility then they cannot accept anything that matters about the Christian faith. As one great Christian thinker pointed out: "Those who assume that miracles cannot happen are merely wasting their time by looking into the texts: we know in advance what results they will find for they have begun by begging the question."[31]

Even among Christians there is great debate about what constitutes a miracle. I do not wish to enter that discussion. However, if we give the briefest definition that a miracle is an event that cannot be explained by natural phenomenon then I think we can demonstrate that belief in miracles is the most logical position to take. Let me point out why, by giving you a formal argument for miracles. This is going to be a regular part of the blog from now on.

1. If a single miracle (as defined above) has ever occurred then we should believe in miracles.

2. At least one miracle has certainly occurred, therefore

3. We should believe in miracles.

Now lets take a look at the argument to see if it holds up. The first premise is somewhat self-evident. If we can show that a

---

[31] C.S. Lewis, *Miracles* (New York: Macmillan, 1947, 1978), p. 4.

miracle has ever occurred then obviously they can occur. Premise number 2 is the controversial statement. How can we say that at least one miracle has certainly occurred?

At present, cosmologists (people who try to figure out how the universe began) have only two possibilities. Either the universe came to exist uncaused, out of nothing at all, or God created the universe. For those who have studied this matter, and feel like there are more ways of looking at this, I encourage you to listen to my debate with Will on BraxtonHunter.com. There really are only two options. The interesting thing is that whichever way the universe began - IT WAS by definition A MIRACLE! Thus, we have at least one certifiable miracle that every individual should believe in no matter her worldview.

The conclusion that "we should believe in miracles" seems logical and acceptable in light of this. Now granted this is an argument for miracles, not the existence of God or truth of Christianity in general, but we are laying groundwork here. In the future I'll explain why the rest of Christianity isn't weird. Still, the next time someone indicates that it's silly to believe in miracles you'll know how to respond.

WHAT'S UP WITH OLD TESTAMENT SACRIFICES?

If there is anything in Scripture that seems weird it is the sacrificial system. Why in the world would God require that mankind do things like kill animals in order to get forgiveness for sin? If animals need to be sacrificed then why did Jesus need to die? Sacrifices are exactly the sorts of things that sometimes cause people to walk away from Christianity and say, "It's just a made up religion." But there really are some good reasons why God requires sacrifices that make sense if you really think.

In Leviticus, Chapters 1-7, there are five types of sacrifices mentioned. The Burnt sacrifices were those in which the entirety of the offering was set on fire and completely consumed by the flames. Grain offerings were those cereal sacrifices of vegetation and produce. Peace offerings differed somewhat in how they were made depending on the circumstances, but they were often voluntary acts of worship. Sin offerings were made on behalf of involuntary sinful acts. That is to say, many times a given Israelite might accidentally violate the law. Trespass offerings were similar, but involved actual money and were specifically made in the event that one man had cheated another (intentionally or not). These few chapters of Scripture outline how and when these offerings are to be made. So, what's the point?

God's requirement of sacrifices in the Old Testament makes sense for two reasons. First, part of what makes God so great is his justice. He must act justly! That means a penalty must be paid for sin. Second, the reason it had to be an animal, vegetation or amount of money is because the penalty must actually cost the sinner something. Thus, we have the sacrificial system. One reason that the Bible is so specific about how the sacrifices were to be done is, undoubtedly, that God wanted to teach obedience to the Israelites. However, we are still left with the question of why Jesus had to die.

Ultimately, the sacrifices that God required of the Children of Israel would not suffice in light of eternity. They were temporary. The system was a sort of "band-aid" solution. The reason for this is that man had sinned against an everlasting God. Often when I preach I point out that if you kill someone's pet (let's say a cat since I'm a dog person), there will be a penalty of some kind. If you kill the owner, however, the penalty will be much bigger. You may go to prison for the rest of your life. In fact, you may receive capital punishment. So there is a small penalty for sinning against an animal and a much bigger penalty for sinning against a man because this is what our own innate sense of justice tells us. So, what must be the punishment for sinning against an everlasting God? Can it be anything but an everlasting punishment? In order to escape everlasting punishment in hell, for sinning against an everlasting God, an everlasting sacrifice must be made.

1. Justice requires that the punishment for sin is equal to the weight of the sin

2. Sin against God is everlasting in weight, therefore

3. The just punishment for sin must be everlasting

The only way this could be done is for God to enter the physical universe and die to fulfill that justice. It all boils down to the fact that God cannot change the fact that he is a God of justice.

He must act justly. This means that a price must be paid. The only just price for everlasting sin is an everlasting sacrifice. Jesus is the everlasting lamb that was slain. To me, this makes perfect sense. The next time it occurs to you, "What's up with sacrifices?" you'll have an answer.

HOW DOES THE TRINITY WORK?

When it comes to the Trinity most of us are naturally inclined to be confused. How could it be that the three individual persons are actually one person? It seems unthinkable and counterintuitive to say that the Father, Son and Holy Spirit are separate and distinct, yet one and the same. Since the fourth century, believers have made every attempt to give a proper analogy for how this relationship works.

Some have claimed that it is not unlike a man who is both a father, a son and a husband. He has three roles, but is one person. Who he is would depend on what role he is filling at a given moment. He is all three at the same time. The problem is that this, if it were true, would mean that the three persons of the Trinity are not distinct persons. In essence, we would merely be calling the same person by three different names. It would also make no sense when compared with the baptism of Jesus, at which time, all three persons were present in different forms (Jesus as the God-man, The Holy Spirit as the dove and the Father as a voice from the heavens). Others have described God as moving from one to the other like an actor wearing different masks. Yet, this meets the same challenges as the aforementioned ideas. So what is the answer?

As I have mentioned in other articles, developments in modern science have demonstrated that what Christianity has always said was true - makes perfect sense. If God exists outside of the universe as its creator, then he cannot be a part of the natural universe. Only in recent years has science determined that there was an ultimate beginning to the universe. Taking this evidence seriously, the Christian knows that the cause of the universe, as the Bible implies, is outside of the natural world. This is God the Father as described in the opening chapters of Genesis. Yet, God wanted to come into the world in order to dwell with man. This is Jesus (God acting in the physical universe). Finally, in order for man (in the physical universe) to be connected with God (outside of the physical universe) he needed a spiritual person to make the connection. This is the Holy Spirit. They are each distinct persons. They are each

God. They are all one.

1. The Father is God outside of the physical universe

2. The Son is God inside the physical universe

3. The Holy Spirit is God bridging the gap

Perhaps the best analogy for this, and it is not original to me, is that of a triangle. Each corner represents a different person of the Trinity. Each corner is a distinct part of the piece, but all are one.

ANGELS AND DEMONS

For some, the idea that there is a supernatural realm of angelic and demonic entities moving all around just beyond the surface of the physical seems like the sort of thing that would be made up by a culture of superstitious barbaric believers in an antiquated religion. However, I think beliefs in angels and demons are perfectly reasonable, but before we get into that let's make it clear just what we mean when we use such terms.

According   to

the *Baker Evangelical Dictionary of Theology* (*BEDT*) an Angel is a,

> . . . superhuman or heavenly being who serves as God's messenger. Both the Hebrew malak and the Greek angelos indicate that these beings also act decisively in fulfilling God's will in the world. But these two terms also apply to human beings as messengers (1 Kings 19:2 ; Hag 1:13 ; Luke 7:24). "Angels" are mentioned almost three hundred times in Scripture, and are only noticeably absent from books such as Ruth, Nehemiah, Esther, the letters of John, and James.[32]

---

[32] Elwell, Walter A. *Evangelical Dictionary of Theology*. (Grand Rapids,

Moreover,

By nature they were spiritual entities, and thus not subject to the limitations of human flesh. Although holy, angels could sometimes behave foolishly (Job 4:18), and even prove to be untrustworthy (Job 15:15). Probably these qualities led to the "fall" of some angels, including Satan, but the Bible contains no description of that event. When angels appeared in human society they resembled normal males (Genesis 18:2 Genesis 18:16 ; Ezek 9:2), and never came dressed as women.[33]

As mentioned above, depending on context the same term that is translated "angel" may refer to a messenger or pastor. Here, we will be referring to angels as one typically thinks of them.

On the other hand, a demon is an angelic being that rebelled against God and is defined by *BEDT* as a,

Spirit being who is unclean and immoral in nature and activities. When demons were created, how they came to be demonic, and their organizational structure are not given significant attention in Scripture because the focus throughout the Bible is on God and his work in Christ rather than on the demonic attempts to demean that work.[34]

While this subject is incredibly interesting, our short purpose here is to explain why belief in angels and demons is understandable

---

MI: Baker Book House, 1984) Print.

[33] Ibid.
[34] Ibid.

and reasonable. So, what's the problem?

Many individuals find it difficult to accept the existence of angels and demons because it would mean accepting belief in supernatural non-human beings. After all, "By nature they [are] spiritual entities. . ." However, if we can demonstrate that God exists, as I have done in previous work [35] (and all over BraxtonHunter.com), then we already have good reason to believe in at least one supernatural being. If we know that one supernatural being exists, then why should we conclude that others can't exist? Think of it this way:

1. If at least one supernatural being exists then it is reasonable to believe in supernatural beings

2. At least one supernatural being does exist (God), therefore,

3. It is reasonable to believe in supernatural beings

Keep in mind, this is not a "proof" that angelic beings exist, but an explanation of why it is reasonable to believe that they do.

---

[35] Check out my books, *CORE FACTS* and *Evangelistic Apologetics*.

So there you have it. The fact that belief in angelic and demonic forces at work in our world is so reasonable is just another reason why so many of us are understandably Christian.

HOW NOT TO TREAT THE BIBLE

I'm not always realistic, but I try. It's something that, for me, requires a lot of work. What I have found to be a necessity for getting to the root of a problem - in my family, work, etc. - is the ability to stop and ask myself one simple question, "What is actually going on here?" For example, last week after preaching in downtown Evansville, IN, a man approached me and said that he was very upset and would likely not be back to that particular church. For about thirty minutes we discussed whether or not one should spank their kids, go to seminary, read books other than the Bible and the nature of hell. The situation was not improving. My new friend was growing more and more adversarial by the moment. I really wanted, as a Christian apologist/theologian/preacher to believe that things really were as they seemed. I wanted it to be the case that the root of all of this was a misunderstanding on his part about some theological or practical Christian issue. If I could only harness the intellectual and spiritual prowess that I had honed over the past fourteen years of study his eyes would be opened and instantly a transformation would occur that would render the man the most agreeable church member in Evansville. That didn't happen. Instead, I asked myself the simple question, "What is actually going on here?" This led to the realization that he had been asked by a member of our church security team not to keep moving in and out of the sanctuary. Only then did I remember that the very individual was constantly in and out of the service charging his cell phone and such. While I usually don't care about this sort of thing, in his case, it had become a huge distraction. Case closed.

However, the same simple question, "What is really going on here," is one I bring to bear on theological and biblical issues as well. I'm immersed in a theolo-geek culture that I love, but that is sometimes characterized by the high-minded, holy-cloud mentality found in the philosophers of Acts 17:21 of whom the bible says, "Now all the Athenians and the foreigners residing there spent their time on nothing else but telling or hearing some new thing." This often leads young Bible-scholars and theologians to erect complex and daunting towers of proof-texts in an attempt to build some new construct or system atop the pages of the sacred text. These begin as theories that serve as fodder for coffeehouse discussions. Then they become alternative hypotheses of interpretation. Next they may become new perspectives as the progenitor of the idea publishes a book on the subject. The final step may or may not involve this formerly bizarre concept being crystalized as doctrine . . . Don't get me wrong this can be a good thing. Sometimes, though very seldom, there is something that has gone unnoticed for centuries that needs to be teased out. Unfortunately, the lust for that holy grail of theology leads to some strange things. Theologians can end up looking less like scholars and more like mad scientists in a lab mixing and stirring various scriptural texts together in an attempt to find some way of elucidating a "truth" that is not there. Alchemy. Often it is in such moments that the scientist needs to remember the hermeneutical principle of asking, "What is really going on here?"

It is at this moment that I should mention that my latest preacher/theologian infatuation involves a man named Brian

Zahnd.[36] Brian took part in a highly publicized debate on Calvinism recently and while some of what he says I cannot help but reject (much to my chagrin), his sermons articulate this principle with words I had not thought to use. He **says**,

> Taking its cues from the scientism of a bygone era, Western Christianity has tried for too long to make the gospel a kind of scientific formula—a pseudo-science of biblical facts, atonement theories, and sinner's prayers—when it's more like a song, a symphony, a poem, a painting, a drama, a dance, and, yes, a mystery.[37]

Now, while I cringe at the preemptive use of the term "mystery," and actually think the "sinner's prayer" would fit well into Zahnd's imagery, (ala the wedding proposal/moment of marriage/invitation and agreement to dance etc.) I agree with him that often we tend to miss the point in an attempt to clinically and lifelessly probe a passage until it gives us either something new, or confirms our latest hypothesis.

I truly don't want to make this a post about Calvinism, but I see it there in *Technicolor*. The story of the Bible is one of choice.

---

[36] Chill out – I don't agree with him on everything.

[37] Zahnd, Brian, Sermon: Modern Man. (http://wolc.com/podcast/modern-man/) Internet. Accessed on 22, January, 2015.

God repeatedly affirms, "If you do this, I will bless you, if you do that I will bring you down." The story of the Bible is one of choice. Without genuine libertarian freedom, there is no genuine ability for sacrifice. Without the genuine ability for sacrifice there is no genuine ability to love. Yet, God is love and commands us to love. Jesus died for every individual in a universal atonement so that anyone who chooses to place her faith/trust in him might be saved. Yet, budding reformation enthusiasts tend to get so pseudo-sciencey with the atonement/sacrificial system and clinically probe and mix enough that they come away with a peer-reviewed limited atonement. Now someone is sure to misunderstand and think that I am saying that an honest exegetical investigation is not necessary or is a bad thing. God forbid! Others might think I am conceding that the most rigid and academic work on the atonement actually does give us a limited one, and we should just ignore that. God forbid! What I'm merely getting at is a clarion call for sobriety in theology. When your work brings you to a conclusion like limited atonement, the best thing might involve asking the question, "Is this really what's going on here . . . Really?"

Lastly, after fourteen years of staying away from this sort of thing for fear of being called a liberal, I'm going to mention a rock song. Secular? You decide. In the year 2000, *U2* released a song called *Beautiful Day* that cleaned up at the Grammys. What most casual fans never heard was an early version of the song called *Always*, that only appeared on the single release of *Beautiful Day*. Remember CD singles? Now you feel old. The song speaks of the need to answer the question, "What is really going on here?" The whole album, that it would have been on, was about the need to remove clutter and cling only to - *All That You Can't Leave Behind*. Because of this, the song uses imagery like "crack the bone - get to the marrow," and "get down off your holy cloud - God does not deal with the proud." *Always* draws to its close with "turn each song into a prayer - now and forever." I had already been thinking of this what's-really-going-on approach to the text when I got in my car and heard the song. I'm not saying God was speaking through a rock band or anything. I'm just saying that the song was in many ways a reminder that truly understanding the Christian faith requires you to be *a student* of the Word *and a lover* of Jesus.

Always

U2

Here today, gone tomorrow
Crack the bone, get to the marrow
To be a bee and the flower
Before the sweetness turns to sour

What we have we're gonna keep, always
What we've lost we don't need, always
What is it that won't let you sleep, always

Be the arrow and the target
Put your head over the parapet
Be uncool, yes be awkward
Don't look in the obvious place
The soul needs beauty for a soulmate

Get down off your holy cloud, always
God will not deal with the proud, always
Well if you dream then dream out loud, always
Eternally yours, always

I want you
I want you
I want you
Touch me now inside
I wanted to be a man
I wanted to call

You say you come to know yourself, always
Don't find yourself in someone else, always
And always wear a safety belt, always
Wait for me I'm running late, always
This is the moment that we share for always

Turn each song into a prayer, always
Now and forever
For always

TALKING PAST EACH OTHER: ONE ISSUE ABOUT THE CALVINISM DEBATE THAT CHRISTIANS MISUNDERSTAND

We don't want to talk past each other! This is a common phrase heard when Calvinists and non-Calvinists discuss their differences. Yet, it almost always happens. One of the primary reasons for this is that many non-Calvinists come to the table already under the impression that their Calvinist brothers do not believe that man is free in any sense. Calvinists constantly speak as though their system allows for free will perfectly well. Is this true? Yes and no.

Broadly speaking, there are three understandings of man's freedom that philosophers speak of when considering the subject:

Determinism - is the view that no free will of any kind exists. Though you feel as though you are making genuine choices it is all an illusion. Determinism is most commonly held by naturalists who believe that the universe is a closed system of cause and effect. Just as the collapse of the first domino in a chain initiates a causal chain in the well placed pieces such that they all come falling down, the determinist believes that even your decisions are the results of chemical reactions in your body and the firing of neurons in your brain. You are not free in any sense . . . at all.

Libertarian freedom - is the belief that man is genuinely free to choose between two options. When you indulge in the chocolate cake rather than heading for the treadmill you experience it as though you made a genuine choice because you actually did make a genuine choice. When you consider your options as though you are free to make a selection among them, you actually are free to make a selection among them. In simple language, libertarian free will is what most people mean everyday when they use the term free.

Compatibilism - What is often considered to be a middle ground position between these two understandings is known as *compatibilism*. Overwhelmingly, Calvinists understand human freedom in this light. On the compatibilist view, man is free to *do* whatever he wants, but not free to *want* whatever he wants. That is to say, man has freedom to exercise his will in accordance with his desires, but he has no control over those desires. This will involve a little illustration.

Imagine that Tom is madly in love with Michelle. The problem is that Michelle is entirely uninterested in Tom. Tom isn't even on her radar, and if left to her own devices Michelle would never love Tom. Yet, Tom is a bright guy. He goes to school to learn chemistry and cracks the formula for the elusive love potion of a thousand fiction tales. Slipping the mixture into Michelle's morning coffee, Tom is fully aware that Michelle will fall madly in love with the first person she sees. He approaches her office just as she takes the first sip of the mysterious brew and they lock eyes. Success! Michelle indeed falls madly in love with Tom. She begins to demonstrate her affections by running her fingers through his hair, bringing him little gifts and batting her eyelashes at every opportunity. She is doing what she wants, but she is not free to want what she wants. The result of the potion is that she is open to suggestion. Tom, by his ploy, has *determined* Michelle's actions by controlling her wants. Is she free? No she is not.

Now since I have offered an analogy that will hopefully appeal to our feminine readers, let me turn to the guys. The greatest film saga ever produced is *Star Wars*. Everyone who has seen the films knows about one of the most quintessential Jedi abilities. It's the "old Jedi mind trick." Thank goodness in Star Wars it only works on "weak minded fools." However, in a fallen world perhaps that's what we all are. Obi Wan Kenobi waves his hand before the enemy and protects his precious robotic cargo with the suggestion, "These aren't the droids you're looking for." The storm troopers, under a trance, reply, "These aren't the droids we're looking for . . . move along . . . move along." Classic. It's also a great example of compatibilism. The storm troopers were saying and doing exactly what they wanted. The problem is that the old Jedi had manipulated them such that they were no longer in control of what they wanted. If you change their wants, then their actions will follow.

So before you stand three options. Either 1) determinism is true and there is no freedom of any kind, 2) libertarian freedom exists and we are genuinely free, or 3) compatibilism is true and you are only free in the sense that you do what you want, but since your wants are chosen for you your actions are determined. Now, a clever reader will have already recognized that there is no substantive difference between 1 and 3. Compatibilism, though its advocates try to argue that determinism is compatible with freedom, just reduces to determinism anyway. Calvinists, however, are compatibilists. This allows them to say, "Free? Of course we believe that man is free. Everyone is free to do whatever they *want*." This is why so many Calvinists and non-Calvinists end up talking past each other.

So is our Calvinist friend right to say that on Calvinism man is free? Yes and no. Man is not free in the established common use of the term. However, if the Calvinist redefines the term free to mean one can do what he wants, but his wants are chosen for him, then yes the Calvinist can get away with claiming that man is free. The problem is that he has to redefine an established term to make this move. When Calvinists say that man is free, they mean something entirely different than actual freedom. Worse, they are actually affirming determinism. On Calvinism, man is simply not free.

In case you think I'm overstating the case, consider the words of John Feinberg of Trinity Evangelical Divinity School. He says, "Calvinists as determinists must either reject freedom altogether or accept compatibilism."[38] There you have it. If one knows how to navigate the language and avoid the (intentionally or unintentionally) deceptive terminology, what is left is naked Calvinism. Naked Calvinism paints human freedom very differently than what most believers know of it from scripture and personal experience.

---

[38] Quoted in - Walls, Jerry L., and Joseph Dongell. *Why I Am Not a Calvinist*, (Downers Grove, IL: InterVarsity, 2004) P. 114.

BLACK MAGIC: A MINOR APOLOGETIC ANNOYANCE ABOUT THE SOTERIOLOGY DEBATE

I'm annoyed about one aspect of the whole Calvinism brouhaha! The debate is an exciting one and many on both sides of the complex biblical/theological/philosophical issue consider it to be vitally important. I do too. I'm an evangelist, and whether or not Calvinism leads to a lack of evangelism it speaks to the nature and mechanics of salvation. This, I think, is the best reason for wanting to dialogue about the subject. However, I have found that there is an unnatural obsession about this issue that causes evangelicals, particularly Southern Baptists, to focus on it to the exclusion of other items that are more pressing for the modern believer. Now, I am greatly appreciative of those who have shared my recent article *Talking Past Each Other,* and I hope that when I write on Calvinism in the future that those same people will again snatch up my thoughts (though I am always humbled and shocked when anyone does) and share them via social media. Still, I offer this caution. The Calvinism debate has become *black magic* that many of us resort to when blog hits are down. If you haven't had many views for a few weeks, just sprinkle a little Calvinism, pro or con, and suddenly the attention comes flooding. The solution is not to stop talking about this vital issue, but rather to start talking as much or more about more important issues.

Atheism/Agnosticism - Whether you are a Calvinist or not, your opponent isn't necessarily going to hell. Atheists and agnostics are and so they warrant more of our time. As a Christian apologist I constantly hear pastors and lay-people say that apologetics is just too hard to learn. I promise you that learning to handle the theistic arguments and the resurrection evidence IS NOT more difficult than learning how to talk about the *ordo salutis*, *transworld depravity*, *compatibilism* or a host of other concepts that arise as the subject of Calvinism is broached. You can learn to do apologetics and if as much effort was put into this as is put into the Calvinism debate perhaps our youth would not be slipping away as freshmen in college.

False doctrine - Now, while there are a great many evangelicals who quietly believe that there opponents in the Calvinism debate are guilty of some sort of heresy, there is no doubt that whether you are Calvinist or non-Calvinist your opponent is a lot closer to truth than Muslims, Mormons, JWs, Hindus, Buddhists, or any other believer in a non-Christian worldview. It is shocking to me that we as evangelicals are putting more effort into rebutting our opponents within Christian soteriological discussions than we are into responding to a false religion like Islam. I personally became convicted about this a couple of years ago and it led me to embark on a yearlong study of Islam for my own apologetic purposes.

Evangelism – I'll say exactly what you would expect from a loud-mouthed, leather-lunged, evangelist. People are dying and going to hell. Reality hit me a few years ago when a former ministry partner called me from his new ministry field on a Native American reservation. He said, "Man, you guys are getting all bent out of shape over Calvinism when I've got people here who I've got to debate with about the alligator god." Look, people need Jesus more than they need John Piper or Kenneth Keathley, and both men would agree.

So, before you sprinkle a little *black magic* into your blog or *Facebook* feed, try asking yourself whether you just did that yesterday. I'm not saying we shouldn't talk about this issue. I personally write on it somewhat regularly, but I try to keep seven or eight other articles or podcasts between my rants on the topic. This is also good advice for those who have become obsessed with some other Christian sub-category. And let's share and retweet articles on other issues that do not directly touch on the Calvinism debate. We do not want to become intoxicated by *black magic*.

TALKING PAST EACH OTHER PART 2 (LOVE)

My previous article on this subject titled, *Talking Past Each Other*, generated quite a bit of heat regarding the Calvinist understanding of human freedom. So much so, in fact, that I wrote a follow-up article explaining that the Calvinism debate has become the *Black Magic* that Calvinists and non-Calvinists both use to generate attention for otherwise slow and unnoticed blogs. The goal should be evangelism, not winning in house debates all the time. In that article I explained that because Calvinism is not a central issue for me, I only write on it occasionally. After every six or seven podcasts, blog articles or videos I complete, I take some space to cover this controversial subject (usually only if I'm asked to do so). However, I also received enough generous comments from those on both sides of the issue to warrant a second installment. I am grateful for those of you who shared that my previous article clarified some of the philosophical language, and I hope this helps as well.

The concept of love (particularly how God loves) is a bit different on Calvinism. On Calvinism God loves the elect. Jesus died and rose again, for the few elect. This means that by definition, God as described by the consistent Calvinist is not omnibenevolent. Of course, a Calvinist could redefine the word "love" as it relates to God and claim that it is "loving" for God to allow those he loves to go to hell when they simply could not choose otherwise. In fact, this is the approach that many Calvinists take.

> D. A. Carson, a prominent Calvinist and scholar, says he is often asked in Calvinist circles, 'Do you tell the unconverted that God loves them?' It's a question, it's a good question Calvinists have to ask, 'cause it's not obvious what they should say to that. His answer: 'Of course I tell them God loves them.' Now on the face of it, I like his answer; but listen quickly, here's what he says: there are three different ways God loves people. First, He loves people by giving them material blessings. Secondly, He loves them by letting the Gospel go out to them, and thirdly, He loves people with electing love. Now here's the point: Carson doesn't know who are the recipients of electing love; he doesn't have a clue any more than I do, or you. Now, can he honestly say with a good conscience, 'Of course God loves you', if all he knows is God is giving you material blessings, if all he knows is God lets the Gospel be preached to you even though you can't possibly respond to it?

Jesus said one time, what is a man profited, if he gains the whole world, and loses his own soul? Let me paraphrase that question: How does the love of God profit a man, even if God gives him the whole world in terms of material blessings, but doesn't give him the grace he needs to save his eternal soul? How does the love of God profit him?[39]

To clarify, what the Calvinist is saying is that there are various senses in which God loves different people. Consider the relationship between the wicked stepmother and the protagonist in the famous story of *Cinderella*. Perhaps the wicked stepmother loved Cinderella in a different sense than she loved her two biological daughters. She made sure there was a roof over Cinderella's head and food in her stomach; she merely wouldn't allow her to attend the ball. Calvinism describes God similarly, but the situation is actually worse. It's not just that Cinderella will not be allowed to attend the magnificent festivities, but she will actually live out her days in the house of the stepmother and then experience everlasting torment while others enjoy an everlasting ball. We must remember, though, that Cinderella's basic needs were supplied for during most of her life. She was given food, clothes and purpose. Isn't this more

---

[39] Walls, Jerry, Walls, J., The Great Debate: Predestination vs. Free Will, (http://theapologeticsgroup.com/product/the-great-debate-predestination-vs-free-will/) Internet. Accessed on 11, September 2014.

Calvinistic stepmother's sovereignty glorious and loving? The answer is no. It is not. The fact is, we would not say about this character that she, in any way, loves Cinderella. Worse still, we would have to determine that one of the most despised villains of all literary works is, in fact, more loving than God. If you have the tendency to rebut the point by noting that Cinderella was portrayed as innocent (as far as the story goes) while man is sinful and undeserving, see my article, *Talking Past Each Other*. Nevertheless, this is the approach that many Calvinists use.

In my debate with a Calvinist professor and pastor in 2013, for instance, my opponent clearly explained:

> If my children as free as they are, run into the street, I will override their freedom and I will not ask them, because I love them in a salvific sense and I choose to set my affections on my children. I help coach their softball team. They're astounding softball players, by the way, and I love all the girls on their team, but not like my two. They're mine. They're mine.[40]

A more honest explanation of the Calvinist understanding that God has different senses in his love could not be imagined. My debating partner loves his own children in a different sense than he loves the

---

[40] Mira, Joe, Braxton Hunter Vs. Joe Mira - *Is Calvinism True,* (http://trinityradio.podomatic.com/entry/2013-10-03T08_03_51-07_00). Internet. Accessed on 11 September 2014).

other children on the team. Naturally. The problem is that I have seldom heard a Calvinist analogy to the nature of God that works, and this one is no different.

The problem is that my Calvinist friend is limited by his humanity. If he could ensure that all girls were loved in the same manner that he loves his own daughters I have no doubt that he would do so. Worse still, his analogy actually does implicate the problem that Calvinism poses for a biblical understanding of God's love. The Calvinist says he would override the free wills of his daughters to protect them from traffic because he loves them in a salvific sense, but he loves the other girls differently (i.e. not in a salvific sense). I'm not even pressing the analogy to conclude that based on his explanation, he would not rescue the other girls on the team since they are not his daughters and he does not love them in a salvific sense. He would, based on the analogy, allow them to die in traffic as he stands watching. Fortunately, from the little I know of this particular Calvinist, I'm quite confident he would do no such thing. He would rescue the other girls on the team just as he would rescue his own daughters.

Now let's imagine what the reaction would be if he followed the implication of the analogy and did not save another girl on the team because he didn't love her in the same salvific sense he loves his own daughters. He stands by watching, as the child is the unfortunate victim of a fatal car accident. He is approached by onlookers who run toward him in fascination and horror. They ask why he did not intervene when he was perfectly able to do so.

His answer, according to the analogy, would be, "I loved the girl, just not in a salvific sense."

"You didn't love her in a salvific sense," we can imagine the bewildered crowd asking.

"No," he might reply, "but don't worry, I do love all the girls on the team, just not like my two."

"Well, how do you love the other girls who are not your daughters," the interrogators demand to know.

The answer would have to be, "I provide them with lemonade and teach them how to play softball, but I do sometimes let them die in traffic accidents."

Now in case you think I'm overstating the Calvinist case, I'm actually infinitely understating. the facts. On Calvinism it isn't a mere traffic accident, as awful as that would be, but everlasting conscious torment. So consider faithfully this simple question about the analogy from my Calvinist debating partner, which is far tamer than the picture from Calvinism, "Would we ever say about the coach who stood by watching an accident that he loved the girls he could have saved?" Would we say he loved them in any sense at all? Of course not. We would say that he was nice to them for a while before allowing them to experience a grisly demise. No amount of lemonade or pep talks could make up for this. We would say he was a monster, or a coward. Again, if you're thinking, "Well, sinners are doing what they want, and they don't want God," or, "God is gracious to save some, while all sinners deserve to go to hell," read my article *Talking Past Each Other*. In the same way Calvin's view of God - who loves some in a salvific sense, wherein he provides eternal life and an escape from death, but blesses others with a few years of rain and crops before damning them choicelessly to everlasting torment - is not loving the unelect in a different sense. He is not loving them at all. He is merely nice to them for a while and then reveals himself to be something else entirely. Yet, Calvinists demand the right to import this definition into some sense of the word *love*. Strange.

If this move is made, then the term love is so far removed from what believers have always thought about God as to require a different word than "love" altogether. Yet, Jesus commands us in Matt. 22:39 to love our neighbors as ourselves and we're to love our enemies - love everyone! If we did that and Calvinism were true, then our love would be more encompassing than God's love. This cannot be. So how can the Calvinist overcome the dilemma? He can honestly admit that, on his view, in no meaningful sense does God love the unelect. To quote from Calvinist Arthur Pink, "God does not love everybody."[41] Until this point is made clear, Calvinists and Non-Calvinists will continue to talk past one another.

---

[41] Pink, Arthur W. (2012-06-18). *The Sovereignty of God* (Arthur Pink Collection) (Kindle Location 373). Prisbrary Publishing. Kindle Edition.

SANTA TEACHES THEOLOGY

The Christmas skirmish is upon us. Whoops. The Christmas season is upon us. Actually, it has been a skirmish, if not a full-blown battle, for the past several years. Don't look at my blog like that. You know exactly what I mean. About this time of the year we begin to hear inflamed opinions from university professors, rabbis, politicians, commentators and Christian pastors. Admittedly, I get irritated by modern attempts to pry "Christ" out of the "mass" of holiday trappings as much as anyone. Vigorously I resisted my compulsion to get on a soapbox at the Chicago International Airport recently when my eyes fell on the words "holiday tree" and simply satisfied myself with a good eye-rolling. Nevertheless, I'm annoyed with the whole conflict. I miss entering this time of year with childlike delight, far removed from the wreckage of colliding worldviews. I know. I was as surprised as anyone. Enjoying spirited debates, I usually welcome an entire month being dedicated to declaring the preeminence of the Christian faith and the reality of the virgin birth in the face of secularism. Maybe this year I'm weary with it all because our daughters, Jolie and Jaclyn, should get to experience it the right way. Don't get me wrong! I'm still in favor of the debate being had. I'm just going to trust all of you to pick up the slack for me this year. I like Santa Claus for what he is and I'm going to let Jolie do the same. However, I found him to be a helpful analogy in a recent discussion.

I have several Christian friends who are "tolerant" of other faiths. When I say "tolerant" I'm not referring to Webster's rendition of the term. I'm using it the way it is meant by left-leaning believers. For them, tolerant is defined as "the understanding that the views of another are equally valid and true." Aren't Muslims, Mormons and Hindus finding truth in their faiths which are just as valid as the truth of Christianity? This was the question recently posed to me. We live in a culture that venerates any belief, no matter how destructive or outlandish, so long as it is labeled a "faith." When I pointed out that many faiths are illogical and all faiths external to Christianity contradict it at some vital point, the questioner explained that faith is different from logic. What she was getting at was the idea that statements of faith don't have to make sense at all. They can be overtly nonsensical, but as she further clarified, as long as they bring hope and peace they warrant the term "true." What I find absurd about this is that we do not respond in this way with regard to any other area of our lives. It would be exciting to spend this blog discussing the problems of relativism, but let's keep Santa in the mix.

The most widespread religious enthusiasm among individuals under the age of ten years old in America is brought about in mid November (at the latest) at the sight of two colors (red and green). Their acceptance of Mr. Claus is completely fueled by faith. I don't know about you, but I see this faith as at least as legitimate as that which fuels scientology. Yet, I do not know (nor have I ever met) a single adult who still truly believes in his existence. Why? Because we know better. We know that certain things are simply not true. Like many false religions, the Santa Claus myth brings great hope. It brings peace. It's wonderful. It just doesn't happen to actually be reality. I submit to you that we should view false religions in the same sense that we view the Santa myth. If they don't happen to be true, then we shouldn't call them true. Moreover, if an individual takes them seriously then we should point all of this out.

I think Santa Claus is awesome! But I think he is awesome in the same way I think Batman is awesome, not in the same way I think Jesus Christ is awesome. One final caveat. I will let my daughters play with Santa dolls, have their photos made with him at the mall and even color pictures of the man. I will not however, let them anywhere near the book of Mormon anytime soon. Merry Christmas!

EVANGELISM

I AM AN EVANGELIST. MY PRIMARY GOAL IN UNDERSTANDING THE TYPES OF THINGS COVERED IN THIS BOOK IS TO REACH UNBELIEVERS WITH THE MESSAGE OF THE CROSS SO THAT THEY MIGHT EMBRACE JESUS. IF THIS BOOK IS MERELY INTERESTING TO YOU, I THINK YOU'RE MISSING THE POINT. LET THIS FINAL SECTION SERVE AS A MOTIVATION TO PUT ALL OF THESE TRUTHS INTO PRACTICE. YOU MAY NOT BECOME A LOUD-MOUTHED, LEATHER-LUNGED, RED-FACED EVANGELIST IN A PULPIT. THAT'S FINE. HOWEVER, WE ARE ALL CALLED TO SHARE OUR FAITH. BECOME A PERSONAL EVANGELIST IN YOUR DAILY LIFE. IN SHORT, SHARE THESE TRUTHBOMBS WITH OTHERS.

SHOULD MINISTERS STILL EXTEND "DECISIONAL INVITATIONS?"

WARNING: Typically I use a good deal of humor in these blogs, but on this occasion I want to warn you that this will be a heavy, direct and controversial discussion.

Poll the average Baptist congregation (and a number of other denominations) on the subject of when and where each member became a Christian and you will hear a myriad of answers. Nevertheless, one that will repeatedly surface sounds something like this, "As the preacher delivered the message, I was convicted. I realized my sin and at the invitation I was one of the first down the aisle. I committed my life to Christ and repented in prayer to God." This "invitation," as it has come to be known, holds a special place in the hearts of many believers in that it was the moment at which they embraced Christianity and truly became followers of Christ. It does not hold a special place for them because of anything about the physical aspects of the event (walking down an aisle, praying a prayer or getting baptized), rather it was the time at which they stood face to face with the reality of their sin, Christ's sacrifice and their need for him, then repented. Has it been abused? Absolutely! There have been many throughout the past several decades who have preached easy-believism, made the church altar itself out to be something holy and even used the invitation for monetary gains. Yet, the question is, "Should we throw the baby out with the bath-water?" In what follows I am going to give a brief defense of the invitation. If you find these words in opposition to your own point of view, you should know that I say none of this with a spirit of anger or sarcasm. On the contrary, I am happy to discuss it with you via email if you would like.

A biblical case for the invitation

In 1 Corinthians 14:24 and 25, just after Paul discusses the dangers related to speaking in tongues in the congregation, he says, "But if all prophesy, and an unbeliever or ungifted man enters, he is convicted by all; the secrets of his heart are disclosed; and so he will fall on his face and worship God, declaring that God is certainly among you." This sounds as though it is a decisional moment wherein an individual who is in one instance described as an "unbeliever" is the next moment proclaiming the existence of the Christian God. It further sounds as though Paul sees this as a desired regular event. One might criticize this interpretation by mentioning that some of the apostolic gifts have past away, but the use of such gifts is precisely what Paul had just finished asking them to limit in the midst of a service.

Acts 8:36-38 describes the meeting between Philip and the eunuch at which time the eunuch had a decisional moment of conversion. I fail to see a clear difference between the eunuch's salvation after hearing the message of Christ and the salvation of an individual in the midst of a congregation inside of a church building. Moreover, in passages such as Matt. 4:19 we read of Jesus extending an invitation to those who heard his message. Further discussion could be had of moments such as the Pentecost event. As I have made this very brief biblical case, I must add one caveat before we move on. If you're a Calvinist, and thus you reject my use of the term "decisional," I invite you to find common ground with me in that from the human perspective we experience our conversion as though it were a libertarian decision whether or not you agree that it is - in fact. I believe that if you can accept that, then you should not have a problem with the above statements.

A philosophical case for the invitation

Blaise Pascal (1623-1662) formulated a quadrilemma argument in favor of belief that is somewhat problematic in the eyes of many today. What has come to be known as "Pascal's wager" is simply an argument that if you are unsure on whether or not to believe in God, it is safer to err on the side of caution and just believe. It is referred to as a quadrilemma because it states four possibilities,

1) If God does NOT exist and I DO believe in him then I will have lost nothing,

2) If God does NOT exist and I DO NOT believe in him then I have lost nothing,

3) If God DOES exist and I DO believe in him I have GAINED everything,

4) If God DOES exist and I do NOT believe in him I have LOST everything.

The point of the argument is that it's safer to believe than it is not to believe. Problems arise for Pascal when one considers that there are a variety of alleged gods, and thus one who is unsure can never be certain he is erring on the side of caution. Also, belief "just in case" doesn't seem to be the kind of belief that scripture calls for. Why do I being the wager up then?

An argument similar to that of Pascal's could be used to make a case for the decisional invitation, that I do not believe makes the mistakes that Pascal's wager does. Perhaps instead of Pascal's wager we could go with "Braxton's best bet." Of course, I don't see it as a bet at all. Simply put, my argument would claim that if the preacher wants to be sure he is honoring God's command in reaching out to the lost, it is safer for him to err on the side of caution and extend the decisional invitation. A note needs to be made in order for you to best see how this argument works. The loudest voice in opposition to decisional evangelism (which by the way is their phraseology, not mine) is coming from those who hold to reformed theological positions. For such individuals (many of whom I have the highest respect for) the reason decisional evangelism is wrong is that it somehow limits the sovereignty of God by allowing man a part in his own salvation. Paul Washer claimed, at a conference for *The Way of the Master*, that the danger of decisional evangelism is that an individual may falsely believe he was saved because he made a decision for Christ and then years later when someone tries to reach out to him he will reject the message because he believes he is already saved based on his decision. But how can this be? If grace is truly irresistible, and libertarian choice is not a determining factor, then I cannot see how Washer's claim that the individual may reject the message based on a prior decision can be valid. Such grace would necessarily be irresistible - no matter what the individual's former church experiences were. So decisional evangelism does not threaten the salvation of anyone. Thus, a quadrilemma argument in favor of it could be stated as follows:

1. If decisional evangelism DOESN'T work and the preacher DOESN'T extend it, the church will have lost nothing

2. If decisional evangelism DOESN'T work and the preacher DOES extend it, the church will have lost nothing

3. If decisional evangelism DOES work and the preacher DOES extend it, the church will have honored God

4. If decisional evangelism DOES work and the preacher DOESN'T extend it, the church will NOT have honored God (in this respect)

To put this in plain language, if grace is irresistible in the sense that reformed theology holds, then decisional evangelism will not hinder salvation (and unless a critic wants to maintain that it is not possible for God to save anyone in the midst of a decisional invitation, it may even be used of God). At most, it will be a waist of time and energy. On the other hand, if decisional evangelism does work, and we don't do it we are not doing everything we could to reach the lost. Which is safer? As my father often put it, "I would rather have God tell me I tried too hard to reach the lost than to have him say I didn't try hard enough."

The hard part for anyone skeptical of this argument is that unless you are %100 certain that you are interpreting scripture properly (meaning you know that decisional evangelism is unbiblical, without a doubt), then you are in danger of erring on the wrong side.

A common sense case for decisional evangelism

Having taken a brief look at the biblical data and the possible philosophical implications, let's take a step back and look at it through the lenses of common sense. Many individuals on both sides of this debate claim that they were born again in the midst of an evangelistic service when they responded at an invitation. Are we really prepared to tell them that they didn't get saved at that point, but some other? This strikes me as absurd and it is also the essence of unbiblical judgmentalism. Moreover, I have known hundreds of individuals who became believers at evangelistic events and went on to be ardent, passionate, changed servants of God. If the concern here is that we might get false converts then it should be mentioned that such a possibility is always present no matter how the church conducts itself. One might say that we end up with a large number of non-Christians in church pews who really never were saved. This is a possibility, nevertheless, were would we want such individuals, but under the strong preaching of God's word regularly?

In order to be justified in passionately preaching against what some have termed "decisional evangelism" one must be able to overcome, not one, but both of the above mentioned arguments and question the testimonies of thousands. If that's what you're into – see you at the altar!

DO ATHEISTS EXIST: EVANGELISM ON FOX'S NEW SHOW UTOPIA

I am often asked whether I believe that any true atheists exist.

It has become a common refrain among believers to say, "I don't

believe in atheists." This is, in my opinion, only half valid. The

pertinent scripture here is Romans 1:18-21 which does indeed speak

of all men in context and explains,

> *18 For the wrath of God is revealed from heaven against all*
> *ungodliness and unrighteousness of men who suppress the*
> *truth in unrighteousness, 19 because that which is known*
> *about God is evident within them; for God made it evident to*
> *them. 20 For since the creation of the world His invisible*
> *attributes, His eternal power and divine nature, have been*
> *clearly seen, being understood through what has been made,*
> *so that they are without excuse. 21 For even though they*
> *knew God, they did not honor Him as God or give thanks, but*
> *they became futile in their speculations, and their foolish*
> *heart was darkened.*

So do atheists exist? Yes and no. The encyclopedia of

philosophy defines an atheist as "One who maintains that there is no God." Now, in a very strict sense, one may maintain that there is no God without actually believing that there is no God. In a very clinical sense, yes atheists exist since there are many people who maintain that there is no God. However, we all know that the question digs a little deeper than that. Whatever we might say about what one maintains, the questioner wants to know whether or not anyone actually believes that there is no God. After all, the passage above does indicate that those who disbelieve are "suppressing the truth" and are "without excuse" because the truth of God's existence is "clearly seen" through what has been made.

Suppression of the truth

On the other hand, anyone who has ever spoken to an honest, seeking, open-minded atheist (yes they exist, but you're not likely to find them in the comments streams on *youtube*) knows that such a person genuinely struggles with the very concept of God. Many of them say they wish they could believe. If you take any one of these people at their word a great problem emerges. Either they are lying to us, or scripture is wrong. Not necessarily.

The fact is that scripture teaches that they are actually lying to themselves. Now, this does not sound all that pleasant to our naturalist friends, nevertheless, one can deceive herself about something without realizing it. In fact, if she realized it the deception would not have been successful. I submit to you that honest atheists are not being disingenuous when they say that they "lack a belief in God." They have convinced themselves that it is true even though that God has revealed himself through nature, and perhaps special revelation in scripture. However, that they suppress the truth becomes clear in many instances.

Behavior of belief

It was recommended to Sarah and I that we watch the new *Fox* show, *Utopia*. I cannot recommend this program for the illicit activities that have become so prevalent among reality television stars. One contestant, however, held my attention and kept me from turning it off. Pastor Jonathan had the self-designated and open goal of reaching and baptizing everyone on the show in Jesus' name. By episode three he already had his first convert. As the group gathered to watch the event two of the outspoken atheists had tears streaming down their faces. How interesting. Why would this be? Why would the power of the image of baptism retain such potency for these unbelievers? In fact, the very convert himself had only days before declared, "there is no Christianity in my utopia!" Fascinating. Could it be that the teary eyed atheists were simply moved by the fact that this was a major event in the life of their fellow utopian? Doubtful. These characters had been open about the fact that they not only saw religion as false, but even a major problem in society. One does not cry at the expression of a major problem in society. They recognized something meaningful and real was happening.

Darkening to deliverance

Like winning lottery prizes hidden beneath a thin layer on a ticket, the veneer of atheism often is scratched away to reveal that atheists know of the God who pursues them. They have been fleeing him all their lives. Nevertheless, they have suppressed the truth to such a degree that they no longer recognize what is happening. But telling an atheist this is often interpreted as condescending. Reaching out to them with rich apologetics, passionate evangelism and the truth of the gospel is the wise choice lest their foolish hearts remain darkened.

So do atheists exist? Yes and no. Yes, there are people who maintain that God does not exist and are not being disingenuous. No, there is no one who has not seen clear evidence for the truth of God's existence.

3 WAYS THE CHURCH SHOULD VIEW ISIS

The minarets seem taller at the moment. Native Jews will tell you that it is traditionally common for mosques in the old city to build towers higher and higher in an attempt to stretch closer to the heavens than other religious structures nearby. Though they sometimes fail in this petty ideological attempt at a physical metaphor for domination, when a mosque is set apart from other buildings and stands alone on a hill it can seem quite mammoth. This is precisely what the world sees in *ISIS*. Indeed, the minarets seem taller at the moment.

As one so-called infidel is cut down after another, the eyes of the world are on black masks with guns and knives. We are primarily concerned with the politics of the situation. Many who are too politically apathetic to hide their fears are honest about their worry of a possible threat for the homeland. As a result, the leader of the free world recently commented:

ISIL poses a threat to the people of Iraq and Syria, and the broader Middle East—including American citizens, personnel, and facilities. If left unchecked, these terrorists could pose a growing threat beyond that region, including to the United States. While we have not yet detected specific plotting against our homeland, ISIL leaders have threatened America and our allies.[42]

We are right to make sure that militarily and politically the world is safe from *ISIS*. However, I was recently struck by a tweet from an American evangelical pastor who commented, "Whatever Jesus said about enemies applies to *ISIS*."[43] Naturally, he was instantly hit with replies from Christians probing for answers. Should we never draw a line in the sand? Should we never protect the innocent? Should we just be pacifists, come what may? Fair questions I think. Nevertheless, In the midst of the firestorm, believers should be as concerned about how the church should view *ISIS* as they are with the reactions of politicians and armies. As for myself, I find it perfectly acceptable to use muscle when necessary and think that it is well within the parameters of the Bible to protect the innocent.

---

[42] Obama, Barak, Statement from the President on ISIL, (http://www.whitehouse.gov/the-press-office/2014/09/10/statement-president-isil-1) Internet. Accessed on 22 January, 2015.

[43] A tweet from Brian Zahnd.

Disagree if you like, but husbands and fathers understand the innate knowledge that it would be objectively wrong and cowardly to allow an intruder to rape and murder their families without attempting defense. Today, though, I'd rather focus on how the church should view *ISIS*.

ISIS needs evangelism - I was horrified following the death of Osama bin Laden that some of the sweetest people I know on Facebook were reveling in the knowledge that the terrorist was "roasting in hell!" Don't misunderstand. I think some level of satisfaction at the realization that justice was done is acceptable. Yet, no Christian should be pleased with the idea of any individual spending an eternity in separation from God. We should wish only that this madman had repented before his death. The same goes for *ISIS*. They need Jesus.

A better picture of Jonah being sent to Nineveh is hard to imagine. What if you were sitting in a cafe in Tel Aviv and received a revelation from God telling you to seek out *ISIS*, march into their camp and proclaim the gospel before swift judgment would come. It would be difficult not to get on a plane headed for whatever modern-day Tarshish you care to visit. Yet, this is the picture of God that we see in the Old Testament. Despite atheist claims that God is a moral monster, he desired the salvation of the Assyrians. I believe He would be pleased and glorified with the salvation of *ISIS*. How this could come about I do not know. However, God is active in this part of the world and for the past several years there have been many Muslims converting to Christianity without even the aid of a missionary as they have been receiving visions of the Lord.

> "There is an end-time phenomenon that is happening through dreams and visions," said Christine Darg, author of *The Jesus Visions: Signs and Wonders in the Muslim World*. "He is going into the Muslim world and revealing, particularly, the last 24 hours of His life - how He died on the cross, which Islam does not teach - how He was raised from the dead, which Islam also does not teach – and how He is the Son of God, risen in power."

> "We receive lots of letters about people who have had dreams about the Lord, visions, even miracles," Shaheen said. "When they watch the program, they say yes, we had a dream or a vision, and they accept Jesus as Lord."[44]

Whatever the possibilities are, and whatever world leaders decide, we must endeavor to view *ISIS* as unbelievers in need of a Savior.

---

[44] Mitchell, Chris, Visions of Jesus stir Muslim Hearts. (http://www.cbn.com/spirituallife/onlinediscipleship/understandingislam/visions.aspx) Internet. Accessed on 22 January, 2015.

ISIS needs attention - Believers should respond to this crisis in part by understanding the belief structure and worldview that has resulted in this group. We are called to "be ready and willing always to give a defense to anyone who asks a reason for [our] hope" (1 Peter 3:15) and we will never be able to do so in evangelistic moments or times of persecution if we do not understand how to defend our views in light of the criticisms of our enemies.

ISIS needs prayer - I am not a pacifist, but I am also not on the front lines of battle. Western Christians can do a great service to the war machine by praying for the swift salvation of *ISIS* so that this problem will be resolved with less bloodshed. If you are rolling your eyes at the thought of praying for repentance among these killers then perhaps you should ask yourself what you believe.

I am fully aware that this may all sound naive. Would I be so cavalier about the idea of seeing *ISIS* saved, or praying for them, if my loved ones had been decapitated on the evening news? I cannot possibly answer that question. Still, this is the greatness of the family of God. When some are not in a frame of mind for such holy activities, others can intercede. *ISIS* represents some of the most wicked arbiters of Allah in the world, but God is willing that none should perish. He desires all to come to repentance. Let the minarets raise crosses.

3 THINGS YOUR CHRISTIAN BELIEFS SHOULD CHANGE

One of my favorite films has always been *Indiana Jones and the Last Crusade*. As a Christian apologist, who is seeking to demonstrate and defend the truth of the Christian message, I can relate to Indy's quest for the supernatural artifact that could turn the world on its head. Though this is one of the most quotable movies in history, my favorite line comes toward the end. Just after the crew arrives at the site of the Holy Grail they discover that not only is the enemy already present, but there are several more challenges that need to be overcome. Only Indiana Jones can successfully procure the sacred cup. Strategically, the film's villain puts a bullet into the stomach of Henry Jones Sr., Indy's father. Now the hero has a choice. He can either spend his father's final moments at his side, or attempt to quickly retrieve the grail on the off chance that it really is a miraculous object that can save his father's life. Faith vs. Naturalism. The villain then says the powerful words, "It's time to ask yourself what you believe."

> *What use is it, my brethren, if someone says he has faith but he has no works? Can that faith save him? If a brother or sister is without clothing and in need of daily food, and one of you says to them, "Go in peace, be warmed and be filled," and yet you do not give them what is necessary for their body, what use is that? Even so faith, if it has no works, is dead, being by itself.* - James 2:14-17

Faith should impact our actions. The Christian message is that there should be some actions that demonstrate the truth of what you believe. Just as Indiana Jones would have remained with his dying father had he not had faith in the grail, we will live lives that testify to naturalism if we do not have faith in the truth of the Christian message. Specifically, three things should immediately change.

1. Personal evangelism - If we don't really believe that Christianity is true, we will never share our faith with others. Conversations like that are awkward. They are awkward because what an individual believes about the big questions of life (where we come from, what the purpose of life is, what happens when we die) are deeply personal. They are awkward because we fear we might sound as though we think of ourselves as enlightened or morally superior. Awkwardness is icky. For that reason we often just don't reach out to others. But it's time to ask yourself what you believe. Is it a true fact about the nature of reality that those who never repent and believe will be sentenced to eternal separation from God? If that's true then it seems unthinkable that we would not preach this message.

2. Peayer - I have my favorite celebrity Christian scholars. If I were told that they were ready to network with me on a regular basis, I would never hesitate to take advantage of that. I would want to talk with them regularly out of appreciation for their interest in my life, to hear direction they might be able to give and knowledge I could gain. The Christian message is that someone far more famous, powerful and wise not only wants to network with you, but bond with, transform and make you. It's time to ask yourself what you believe. If the message is true, it seems foolish to let that opportunity pass.

3. Bible study - We ingest the thoughts of others everyday. You're doing it right now. Yet, the creator of the universe has given you a volume of material that is universally agreed upon by Christians to be the most powerful collection of documents on earth. It has the power to provide you with insight into every subject. It's time to ask yourself what you believe. If you really believe that the message is true, how could you let a day go by without reading from the Bible?

If you are reading this blog article then I believe that you believe that you believe. Read that again very slowly. Just because you believe you believe, doesn't mean you believe *in fact*. If we all really believed the message as much as we say we do, wouldn't our lives look a little different? If you are already doing these things, "you have chosen . . . wisely."

WHAT WOULD THE MARTYRS SAY: MY BELATED FOLLOW-UP TO THE WWJD CRAZE

Universally, the most popular jewelry for anyone of any social status for the last several years has been the rubber bracelet. Twelve year olds, rock stars, preachers and presidents can be seen, the world over, wearing otherwise commonplace jewelry which is specific to their position with the exception of a simple colored band. This relatively new construct has ensured that we all wear our hearts on our wrist (if not our sleeves). I actually like this idea. In some cases it has become as easy as glancing down as you shake hands with a new acquaintance to discover what matters the most to them. Yet, before Lance Armstrong exploded the fad into a phenomenon, many church-going teenagers could be seen (particularly in the late 90's) with, the now institutionalized, WWJD bracelet. What would Jesus do? A fascinating, but basic question.

However, it recently occurred to me that a similar question might retain more potency for the modern believer. "WWTMS?" I know, I know. It has one too many syllables to really catch on. But I would ask "What Would The Martyrs Say?" Naturally, for a Christian the questions of what Christ himself would think or do in a given situation should be paramount. The problem is that the details of our Savior's death, burial and resurrection (not to mention his teachings) have become so commonplace to His followers that, whether we like it or not, many of us have become desensitized to the whole matter.

Famously, the church father Tertullian claimed that the blood of the martyrs is the seed of the church. Put flatly, the willingness of early believers to die for the veracity of their claims, spurned on the growth of the church. They took it seriously. They spoke boldly. When and how they were killed spoke volumes to others. We would not have the message, the scripture, the numbers or the history that we know have if it were not for their sacrifices. Our Christian heritage is priceless.

This all occurred to me recently when I was talking to a friend and he mentioned that if someone has unchristian beliefs he simply "appreciates the diversity" of his social circle. "I'm just not the type of person to discuss, debate or try to convince others that my faith is right," he said, before following with, "I'm not what I would call liberal, but I'm probably not conservative either." Wow! It is true that with statements like that, you will have a large and diverse community of friends. You would also be welcome to say something like that on *The View*. Katie Couric might even give you a welcoming nod and wink of approval from behind her desk at *CBS Evening News*. But ask yourself, "WWTMS?"

Our spiritual ancestors bled and died grisly deaths so that we could know the way of salvation and have communion with the Messiah. What would they have to say to comments such as those mentioned above? After being devoured by lions, sewn into burlap bags filled with venomous serpents, being cast into the sea, or beheaded by some gladiator, I doubt they would share such sentiments. Before you click the address bar to navigate away from this page and look at youtube videos of cute puppies, or head off to that trendy coffee shop, stop and consider what this means. Ask yourself the question, "Do I take my faith seriously?"

By the way, "Live Strong!"

Made in the USA
Las Vegas, NV
25 July 2023

75210156R00118